Kids on the Brink

Understanding the Teen Suicide Epidemic

by
David B. Bergman, M.D.

THE PIA PRESS

This book is not intended to replace personal medical care and/or professional supervision; there is no substitute for the experience and information that your doctor or mental health professional can provide. Rather, it is our hope that this book will provide additional information to help people understand the nature of adolescence and psychiatric conditions that can evolve.

Proper treatment should always be tailored to the individual. If you read something in this book that seems to conflict with your doctor or mental health professional's instructions, contact him/her. There may be sound reasons for recommending treatment that may differ from the information presented in this book.

If you have any questions about any treatment in this book, please consult your doctor or mental health care professional.

In addition, the names and cases used in this book do not represent actual people, but are composite cases drawn from several sources.

For information write:
Psychiatric Institutes of America,
part of the National Medical Enterprises Specialty Hospital Group.
1010 Wisconsin Ave. NW
Washington, D.C. 20007

Contents

Dedication

To my daughters, my best teachers and guides.

Acknowledgments

I would like to thank Sandra Strain, my friend and secretary, and Chris Landsittel, Southwood's professional staff coordinator, for their able assistance. I am also grateful to Gretchen Burns for her comments and support. Finally, I'd like to acknowledge Marilyn Devroye, without whose involvement this book would not have been possible.

About the Author

A graduate of Harvard Medical School, Dr. Bergman trained in general and adolescent psychiatry at the Albert Einstein College of Medicine. Currently an Associate Clinical Professor of Psychiatry at UCSD, he has also held faculty positions at Einstein, as well as at the Medical College of Georgia. A past President of the San Diego Psychiatric Society and a Fellow of the American Psychiatric Association, Dr. Bergman has been Medical Director of Southwood Hospital and Residential Treatment Centers since 1976.

PART ONE

WHAT'S BEEN HAPPENING TO OUR KIDS?

1

Adolescent Suicide: An American Tragedy

In the photograph taken by her mother, five-year-old Jane is high in the air and her father is pushing the swing; both are grinning hugely. Anyone looking at that photo would assume this happy little girl, secure in her parents' love, would sail through adolescence and mature into a radiant young adulthood.

Instead, the story ended tragically. Jane took her own life at the age of 19. What on earth happened?

From a psychiatrist's point of view, the story has a poignant familiarity. Little Jane was indeed a loved and happy child, energetic on the playground and bright in the classroom. It was true that from her lawyer father, whom she adored, she felt tremendous pressure to achieve. Outwardly, however, she seemed to thrive on the challenge. As she grew older she did beautifully in both school and sports, making the honor roll every semester and leading her high school swim team to the state championship.

In her freshman year of college, Jane decided she wanted to be a doctor; she set out to get top marks so she would be accepted by the best medical school. A few months into her sophomore year, her friends began to comment on how obsessive she was about getting straight As. She haunted the library, studied late into the night, and spent less and less time socializing.

After spending that year's Christmas break with her family, Jane came back to college and unpacked her bags. She had a snack at the student center and then checked her campus mailbox, where she found her grades for the first semester. Slowly she walked back to her room, studying the computer-printed report. She sat down, wrote a short, neat note on shell-pink stationery, sealed it in a matching envelope, left it on her desk, and took a walk into town. She rode an elevator to the top of the highest office building, climbed a fire escape to the roof, mounted a low concrete wall—and did a swan dive to her death seven stories below.

Jane's suicide note read simply:

> Dear Mom and Dad,
> I love you. I'm sorry I got a B in chemistry.
> Jane

At the age of 19, Jane had taken her own life. The meaning behind her act was complex: deep disappointment in herself for failing to achieve her own goal of straight As; fear of a critical reaction from her parents, especially her father; hidden rage and hopelessness at feeling she had to meet impossible expectations. Her parents, of course, were absolutely devastated by her death. Though they tried to pick up the pieces of their lives, they could not help blaming themselves and each other harshly and remorselessly. Four years after Jane died, their marriage dissolved.

Teen Suicide in the United States

Was Jane's suicide typical? Yes and no. As the medical director of Southwood Hospital, in the San Diego area of California, I work with large numbers of teenagers, including many who are suicidal when they first come for treatment. In addition, I frequently counsel parents of youngsters who have attempted or actually committed suicide. Over the years, I've learned that only some of the kids who kill themselves are like Jane: high achievers devastated by a seemingly minor setback. Many others come from completely different backgrounds, have entirely different motives for suicide, and choose very different ways to die.

It's a chilling fact that suicide, by various means, is *the third leading cause of death* for American kids aged 15 to 24; only accidents and homicides rank higher. What's worse, doctors know that many deaths that appear to be accidents and homicides are really suicides in disguise. Adolescents are the only age group in the United States for which the suicide rate has been on the rise.

From the mid-1950s to the mid-1980s, the American youth suicide rate more than *tripled:* from 4.1 suicides per 100,000 kids in 1955 to 12.5 suicides per 100,000 kids in 1984. Between 1970 and 1980, according to the Centers for Disease Control, one of every six Americans who committed suicide was a youngster aged 15 to 24. Statistics for younger teens were sketchier, but figures for the group aged 10 to 14 show that suicide rates for these kids rose by 32 percent between 1968 and 1978.

Youth suicides rates in our country remain appallingly high. Every day, some 14 youngsters take their lives, which adds up to *5,200 adolescent suicides per year.* And with every passing hour, some 30 kids attempt to commit suicide: That's *more than 700 adolescent suicide attempts per day.*

Young people discover many paths toward self-destruction. Those inclined to violence (most of them boys) shoot themselves, hang themselves, jump from high places, or hurl themselves in front of moving cars or trains; some seek death through reckless driving or gang warfare. Those who shun violence (including many girls) opt for drug or medication overdose, asphyxiation by gas or car exhaust, or wrist cutting.

According to some surveys, up to 41 percent of kids of high school age have thought about suicide, and as many as 10 percent may be at risk for suicide. For college-age students, suicide rates more than doubled between 1968 and the 1980s; in this age group, suicide as a cause of death rose from fifth place in the early 1970s to second place in the late 1980s.

The news is not all bad: the teen suicide rate seemed to level off in the mid-1980s. Yet as of this writing, the rate of suicides per 100,000 teenagers was still more than twice that of 1960. Faced with these heartbreaking statistics, and thinking of the thousands of families each year who are stricken by the tragic loss of a beloved adolescent son or daughter, we naturally ask: What on earth has been going on? Why, over the last three decades, have our youngsters been taking their own lives in record numbers? And what, if anything, can we do about it?

The Meaning of "Suicide"

According to the *Oxford Dictionary,* the word suicide was first used in the year 1651; before that time, the idea of killing oneself was a very rare concept. Unfortunately, we are all quite familiar with the concept today. Yet health professionals are still surprisingly divided on the question of what counts as suicidal behavior. Consider, for example, the emaciated young woman with anorexia nervosa, whose severely disturbed eating pattern amounts to self-starvation: Should she be called suicidal, even though she says she does not want to die? Or take the young man who discovers that a few seconds of oxygen deprivation can enhance orgasm during masturbation: When he overdoes it one day and dies by strangulation, does his death by "autoerotic asphyxiation" count as a suicide?

For the purposes of this book, I will confine the

definition of suicidal behavior to actions taken by young people who *consciously, although perhaps only momentarily, intend to kill themselves.*

Why Suicide?

People used to assume that any youngster who committed suicide, or tried to, had to be mentally ill. But the issue is not that simple.

First, many kids who are diagnosed as having a mental illness are not suicidal. In fact, one study showed that profoundly disturbed mental patients, suffering from schizophrenia or psychosis, were somewhat *less* likely to commit suicide than patients whose mental disturbances seemed less severe.

Second, some teens who have committed suicide, or tried to, showed no signs at all of severe mental or emotional disturbance before their suicidal act.

It's true, however, that most suicidal people, whatever their age, are very depressed and unhappy, struggling with feelings of isolation, alienation, rage, despair, and hopelessness.

In my work with adolescents at Southwood Hospital, when I probe for the meaning behind a particular suicide or suicide attempt, I generally find one or more emotional themes at work. Some common themes, as seen by therapists who work with these youngsters, are: *self-murder, retaliatory abandonment, control over the death process, reunion,* and *rebirth.* Let's take these one by one and see what's behind them.

Emotional Themes of Adolescent Suicide

(1) Self-murder.... Perhaps the most common of all teen suicide themes is that of self-murder: the ultimate form of self-punishment. Kids in this frame of mind are driven by a sense of guilt, worthlessness, and hopelessness. Jane's suicide, which we saw at the beginning of this chapter, was partly based on her self-murderous feelings.

Fortunately, teens who feel like murdering themselves don't always succeed. The story of a boy I'll call Mack is a clear example.

Mack's Story

Mack was an only child. His father was a career military man; his mother, who was chronically depressed, had been a patient of mine for several years. Bright and cheerful as a young child, Mack became rebellious and defiant at the age of 12 as the changes of puberty began. His grades dropped, he misbehaved at school, and when tensions mounted at home he manipulatively played his strict father and his indulgent mother against each other.

Mack's mother, concerned about her son, brought him to see me on several occasions. Because I felt the boy was depressed, I prescribed antidepressant medication and referred him to another therapist who also worked with youngsters. Mack, however, resented going to therapy and resisted the therapist's efforts to reach him.

Meanwhile, Mack had found a best friend: a younger boy who looked up to him as an "older brother" and role model, and whom Mack, by this time 14 years old, treated almost like a puppet. One day Andy, the younger boy, stole some money from his mother's purse and told Mack about it. To his surprise, Mack criticized and berated him.

Hurt and defiant, Andy then ran away from home and remained away for a full day, a night, and part of the next day. While he was gone, Mack sank into guilt and remorse. He blamed himself for having cruelly driven away his best friend, and he began to obsess on the idea that Andy would somehow get killed. He refused to eat or sleep, and he cried so inconsolably that his mother made an extra therapy appointment for him. When she got home from work to pick up her son and take him to the appointment, she found a suicide note on the boy's desk—and Mack sitting in the master bedroom, holding his father's loaded revolver to his face.

Fortunately, the mother arrived in time to prevent her son from killing himself. Mack was hospitalized, did well in the adolescent treatment program, and went through the rest of his teen years relatively smoothly. Here was a young man who almost committed suicide out of guilt and a wish for self-punishment, but who was lucky enough to emerge intact.

(2) Retaliatory Abandonment...Kids who feel emotionally betrayed by those they depend on sometimes think of suicide as a way to hit back or get even. Lois' suicide was an example of this theme.

Lois's Story

Lois, aged 16, dark-haired and vivacious, was having more and more arguments with her parents over issues of freedom and independence. The focus of the problem was her boyfriend, George, who was also 16. Lois's mother, who came from the Philippines, was very religious, and had strict parochial values and morals; she was convinced that Lois and George had a sexual relationship. She pressed her daughter to stop seeing George, and when that failed, she shamed and scolded Lois constantly, set strict evening curfews, and refused to speak to George or allow him in the house. Lois's father went along with his wife.

Lois and George were indeed having sex, and eventually Lois got pregnant. When she confessed this to her parents they shouted and wept, forbade her ever to see George again, and restricted her to the house after school and on weekends. Because of their religious beliefs, they did not suggest or even consider the possibility of an abortion. Lois herself did think of abortion—but because of her upbringing, the thought filled her with unbearable guilt.

Devastated at disappointing her parents, enraged at being caught in a lie about her sexual activity, frightened at the thought of pregnancy, and confined to her home with nothing to distract her, Lois withered. For ten days she cried, ate almost nothing, refused to speak, and slept poorly. On the eleventh day she slipped out of the house, walked straight to a 50-foot-high boat-access pier, strode to the end, and leaped off.

Lois was lucky: Lifeguards plucked her from the choppy water before she drowned, and hospital emergency personnel referred her for psychiatric evaluation. Her parents, who actually did care deeply about her, were shocked, remorseful, and very grateful that she was still alive. They willingly entered therapy with her.

Lois felt her parents were systematically crushing her spirit, punishing her for getting pregnant. Suicide occurred to her as a way to get back at them for hurting, humiliating, and oppressing her.

After talking things over with a therapist and her parents, Lois, now two and a half months pregnant, decided on an abortion. By this time her parents realized that she was growing up, and that she desperately needed to separate from them and make some decisions for herself. They still felt abortion was wrong, but they agreed the decision was hers to make. Lois had the abortion, and her relationship with her parents matured. She went on to graduate from high school, and later got her own apartment and managed to handle both college and a job.

(3) Control Over the Death Process....Some suicidal teens flirt with death not because of depression or obvious, crushing problems, but because they are obsessed with gaining control over every aspect of their life—even its ultimate conclusion.

If you have ever read any how-to literature for parents of teenagers, you know that all adolescents face a major task: leaving childhood dependency behind and developing an adult sense of autonomy and responsibility. The road is usually rocky and littered with obstacles. Kids are impatient with structure and discipline, while parents are reluctant to relinquish control.

In their search for increasing control, most teens test the limits through arguments with parents and teachers: how late at night they can stay out on a date, when they can have the car, what topics make suitable themes for school newspaper articles, what kind of behavior deserves a detention.

Other teens, though, carry their search for control to dangerous extremes. From watching TV or the movies, most of us are familiar with "chicken," the so-called game in which automobile drivers head toward a cliff or each other—and the first one to put on the brakes is the loser. We've also watched professional actors portray Russian roulette: A person with a partially loaded gun points it at his head and squeezes the trigger, while others make bets on whether the chamber will prove empty or full.

These death-defying acts, eminently foolhardy and irresponsible, are classic adolescent-style bids for omnipotence. A flirtation with death, a narrow escape from disaster, produces a momentary high: a feeling of power and mastery, a sense of winning in the struggle to adulthood. The youngster who's prone to foolish risk-taking feels, at least dimly, that the events shaping his life are beyond his control. He sees a desperate, daring risk as a chance to act, to *gain some measure of control* over life, even if it means dying in the process—which, tragically, sometimes happens.

The Brown University Cyanide Vote

It's a mistake to underestimate the depth of young people's desire to control every aspect of life, including its final outcome. Some years ago at Brown University, an Ivy League school, students voted overwhelmingly in favor of a proposal that the college infirmary stock cyanide pills. The rationale? When nuclear disaster struck, as students felt it eventually would, anyone who wanted to could commit suicide by taking cyanide, rather than face the horror of living in a world poisoned by radiation. If they couldn't control life, the students reasoned, they could at least control death. (In 1990, however, a spokeswoman for Brown University health services stated that the infirmary never did acquire the cyanide pills, and had no plans to do so.)

(4) Reunion.... In literature, *Romeo and Juliet* is the best-known example of the reunion theme: the fantasy that suicide will enable a person to join a loved one who has died or will soon die. Unfortunately, real-life teenagers sometimes fall for this kind of wishful thinking. Perhaps it's a boy who has lost his father or a deeply loved uncle. Perhaps it's a girl devastated by the death of the rock star she idolized. Perhaps it's a group of friends of a youngster who died tragically through suicide, accident, or illness. Or perhaps it's a pair of star-crossed lovers (just like Romeo and Juliet) who sign a suicide pact, swearing that life has become too difficult to bear and that neither one wants to live without the other.

Adults are sometimes swayed by the romantic fantasy of reunion through death: Suicides increased briefly but noticeably, for instance, after the death of Marilyn Monroe and the assassination of John Lennon. But it's teenagers who seem particularly apt to glamorize and romanticize suicide; a number of "cluster suicides" have occurred among high school students over the past decade. A partial explanation of cluster suicides is that some adolescents seem not to understand the utter finality of death.

(5) Rebirth....In my experience, the idea of rebirth through suicide occurs mainly to adolescents who are severely mentally disturbed and/or psychotic. The rebirth idea itself is not new, of course; Hindu philosophy, widespread in Asia, includes the idea of reincarnation. In the Hindu scheme, however, suicide is actually a step downward on the incarnation ladder.

Occasionally a mentally ill adolescent whose mind tends toward grandiose or bizarre thinking, and who may have absorbed bits and pieces of oriental philosophy, seizes on the idea of suicide as a gateway to rebirth into a nobler, better, higher form of life. This kind of delusional thought may also result from physical brain disease, or it may arise under the influence of drugs and alcohol.

Cry For Help?

As these various emotional themes illustrate, there is not one simple explanation for teenage suicides and suicide attempts. It's important to realize, however, that whatever their motives for wishing to die, most young people who contemplate suicide are highly ambivalent about death right up to the moment of their suicide attempt. Significantly, only a small percentage of adolescents who try to commit suicide actually die. Many kids who attempt suicide leave a window of opportunity for rescue:

- They take an overdose of pills, but they do it in front of friends who will probably tell.
- They slit their wrists, but they do it at home between 3 p.m. and midnight, so that a family member will probably discover them in time.
- They sit in a garage with the car engine running, but they leave the garage door partway open so that some oxygen will still reach them.

The window-of-opportunity phenomenon suggests that many teen suicide attempts are really cries for help. That's why I believe that education about adolescent suicide can help create a climate of prevention. Whether you are a parent, a teacher, a health professional, or a teenager, the more you understand about suicide, the greater your chances of spotting a suicidal kid and intervening in time to prevent a tragedy.

Social Change: The Facts Behind the Statistics

This brings me back to an earlier question: Why did the adolescent suicide rate triple from the 1950s through the 1980s? It's my feeling that a large part of the explanation lies in the profound changes in American life that occurred during that period.

From the advent of commercial air travel, through the threat of nuclear annihilation, to the dawn of the electronic age, the old, familiar world has literally transformed beyond recognition in the span of a single lifetime. Simply stated, too much in our daily life changed, and changed too fast. Even for adults, the result was intellectual and emotional confusion. For sensitive teenagers, struggling to come of age in a world nobody fully understood anymore, the psychological climate was one of anxiety and depression. Many of them, groping for meaning, saw suicide as a way out—quite literally, a way to kill uncertainty.

Social theories of suicide are nothing new. As far back as 1856, a French researcher named Brierre de Boismont questioned 265 people who had planned or attempted to take their own lives. From their answers, he concluded that suicide occurs "as a consequence of changes in society leading to social disorganization and to alienation for many people." Some 40 years later, the social theorist Emile Durkheim agreed. Suicide will not be prevalent, Durkheim wrote, in a society that is politically, economically, and socially well integrated.

Early in this century, Freud theorized that suicide was predominantly an individual problem: a shifting of the balance of power between the person's Eros, or life instinct, and Thanatos, or death instinct. Later psychoanalysts also assumed the causes of suicide lay within the individual's own psyche.

As I've said, teenagers attracted to suicide may be motivated by any of a number of psychological themes. But I think it's also useful to step back and see the stage upon which the drama unfolds. We need to understand the pushes and pulls of our social environment that bring these themes to the surface.

Inevitably, young people sense and react to the impact of rapid, radical social change. They first feel it keenly in the family, which introduces them to life and teaches them how to live. And later on they feel it in the outside world, that vast, frightening, and alienating arena where they are eventually expected to function as adults.

In the next two chapters I'll be discussing the ways in which profound changes, both in the family and in the outside world, have scrambled the rules of the game of life for the modern American adolescent, setting the stage for the abnormally high rate of teenage suicide we have seen over the past three decades.

2

Home Used to Be a Cozy Place

Think back, if you can, to the emotional quality of life in the 1940s and 1950s. If you're not that old, spend a minute contemplating a Norman Rockwell painting, and try to sense the mood of the times.

Back in those long-gone days, when the radio was the centerpiece of family entertainment, family life was . . . well, claustrophobic, by today's standards. But at least it was peaceful: regular, ordered, and predictable. You could take quite a few things for granted.

Were you born on a farm? Then chances are you were expected to grow up and work your own farm someday. Were you a small-town kid? Then you probably saw your future in that self-same town, or one nearby. You were *from* somewhere, and that shaped your identity, your loyalties, and even the way you talked.

If you were a boy, you probably looked to your dad, or some other male relative, for vocational inspiration. He worked for the steel mill? Then maybe you would, too. He sold insurance. Then he could probably introduce you to that line of work. He was a lawyer? There was a good chance you would follow in his footsteps.

If you were a girl, your mom's life accurately portrayed your own future. You would marry, probably soon after you finished your schooling, and begin your life as a homemaker. You would bear children. You would knit and sew for them, and read them stories, and cook, and clean, and wash, and mend, and decorate the house, and entertain.

In the pre-1960s, life was traditional and calm. It had a quiet, peaceful, ordered quality that today is difficult to imagine, let alone remember.

The Shrinking Family

Even in that idyllic era, however, the breakup of the extended family—that warm, intimate assembly of two or three generations living under one roof or at least in close proximity—was well under way. The gradual demise of the extended family deprived vulnerable children and teens of emotional support. It left them wide open to loneliness, self-doubt, and, yes, thoughts of suicide.

These days, we have to look into the hidden ethnic pockets of America to find people living in extended families. For most of us, "family" means nothing more than a child or two living with a parent or two. But in the old days the family was quite different: a lively, cozy gathering where children and their parents commonly shared living space with grandparents, unmarried aunts or uncles, and others.

A study of life in Massachusetts at the turn of the century showed that 90 percent of the households had *three or more adults:* both parents, plus a grandparent, a maiden aunt or a bachelor uncle. "Mothering" was definitely a mother's job, but Mom was not alone: The other adults in the family casually did their share of nurturing, too. A child growing up in an extended family was never short of people to watch her, take an interest in her, advise her—and criticize her, too. She knew who she was, and she knew how to seek comfort in her relations with others. If she was on the outs with her mother, she could go to her aunt or her grandmother for conversation, consolation, and a fresh point of view.

All this changed as American society mobilized, speeded up, and spread out. With the country changing from an agricultural to an industrial economy, more and more young men and women left the countryside to find work in or around the city. Grandparents stayed behind on the old homestead, hundreds or even thousands of miles away from the new grandchildren being born. Unmarried sisters and brothers found their own city apartments. The nuclear family—two parents and their children—became the modern norm. A family was likely to live in one place for a few years and then, because of a corporate promotion or reassignment for the father, pick up and move to an entirely different city or state. Life for mothers and children got lonelier. Henceforth, a kid who wasn't getting along with her mother had no one to turn to except, perhaps, her friends. If she didn't have friends, her life was depressingly solitary.

More Family Trauma: Divorce

As if the new isolation were not enough, the nuclear family itself began to disintegrate. Rates of divorce started to climb in the 1950s, as traditional ideas of commitment gave way to vague new notions about freedom and personal fulfillment. Chillingly, the *rates of divorce and of teen suicide climbed in tandem, tripling over the next 20 years.*

Currently, the United States has the dubious distinction of holding the world's highest divorce rate: One of every two American marriages eventually splits up. This is troubling in itself; what's worse, several reliable studies show that most youngsters who commit suicide are children of divorce.

- In the book *A Cry for Help,* Dr. Mary Giffin cites a study in which 71 percent of the young people who had attempted suicide came from broken homes.
- Los Angeles psychiatrist Joseph Teicher found that 72 percent of a group of young Californians who committed suicide lived in a home where one or both parents were absent; 58 percent had a parent who had been married more than once; and 84 percent of those with stepparents wanted the stepparents to leave.
- At New York's Bellevue Hospital, two-thirds of 102 teens who attempted suicide lived with only one parent or with neither parent.
- In Toronto, over a period of 70 years, 505 young people were treated for attempted suicide; more than half of them came from a family with an absent parent. In a quarter of the absent-parent families, *both* parents were gone.

Why the strong correlation between divorce and adolescent suicide? Mental health professionals believe that, in many respects, divorce is harder on a child than the death of a parent. As Dr. Giffin wrote, "Death is final—an irrevocable separation. Divorce means torturous memories lingering for years, the beloved parent dropping in and out of a child's life, and the child's terrible fear that he was somehow responsible for the split; that if his parents really loved him, they would have stayed together."

Studies show that the older the child is when her parents divorce, the worse she tends to fare psychologically. Since she has considerable self-awareness, the older child is apt to blame herself for the breakup of her parents' marriage. Since she can understand cause and effect, she knows the divorce is responsible for the new discomforts in her life: less parental attention and supervision, less money to live on, and—if the parents share custody—a disturbing sense of transience as she shifts back and forth between two households. She is apt to carry with her a lingering feeling of hurt, loss, and betrayal. No wonder she's at increased risk for suicide.

"God Is Dead"

Demise of the extended family, isolation of the nuclear family, splitup of the family through divorce—along with all this, there was yet another assault on the integrity of the household: the loss of the influence of religion on family life.

Before World War II, organized religion was the typical family focal point. Protestant families had Sunday and midweek worship services, church school for children, a young people's meeting, Bible study for adults, potluck suppers, mission and charity projects: a full social agenda. Catholic families had obligatory Mass on Sundays and other holy days, weekly confession, meatless Fridays, CCD sessions or perhaps parochial school for the children, novenas, rosaries: a colorful palette of required activities. Devout Jewish families had the *mezuzzeh* nailed to the door, *yarmulkes* for men and boys, strict kosher dietary laws, candlelight on the eve of the Sabbath, Friday nights and Saturdays at the synagogue and without car travel or electricity, passionate discussion of the fine points of religious law: a rich blueprint for living.

Inexorably, as the American social centrifuge spun families down into units as small as one parent and one child, religion lost its hold on most people. Swayed by new scientific theories about the origin of the world and the nature of the universe, many parents could no longer accept religious teachings literally. Intrigued and exhilarated by the ever-present entertainment of movies and television, parents and their children drifted away from religious-based social activities. Mainline religious institutions, eager to keep step with the times, reduced their demands on behavior—and thus relinquished much of their moral authority. In the 1960s, "God is dead" became a trendy social statement. God may not have been dead, but traditional religious life was certainly ailing.

Bringing Up Children: A Job For Experts

With organized religion fast losing status and influence, even parents who still looked to the clergy for personal inspiration went elsewhere for advice on how to bring up the kids. Science seemed to be usurping religion's authority to explain and interpret life. Medical doctors and psychologists, whose prestige was steadily increasing, became the new child-rearing experts: Mothers eager for guidance pored over how-to books by Benjamin Spock, Bruno Bettelheim, Arnold Gesell, Haim Ginott, Eda LeShan, and others.

What they read made them uneasy, for most of the new oracles of parenting—inspired at least partly by Sigmund Freud's theory of the unconscious—were quick to blame Mom for anything that went wrong with the children. Was the son rigid and fearful? Mother had obviously toilet-trained him too early and too harshly. Was he rebellious and destructive? Mother was not listening to his real needs and wants. Was the daughter timid and bashful? Mother had surely undermined her self-confidence. Was she a poor student? Mother had failed to motivate her.

Anxious about the possibility of stunting or warping their children's development, mothers in the 1960s followed the experts' advice and became increasingly permissive; dads, absent from the home anyway except for a few hours in the evening, went along with the trend. In many households, younger kids no longer had bedtimes, and older kids no longer had curfews. Parents questioned the wisdom of subjecting their children to the regimentation of public school; books like A.S. Neil's *Summerhill* extolled the virtues of the "open school" that scorned both schedule and curriculum. Teens themselves, of course, were quick to agree that chores, house rules, and school discipline would harm their developing psyches.

The era of overly permissive child-rearing produced a large number of confused, aimless, self-absorbed kids who had great difficulty moving beyond adolescence into the adult phase of their lives. As this trend continued, so did the rise in the adolescent suicide rate. By the 1970s, Dr. Spock himself—appalled by the drug abuse and social disorganization of the hippie era—had recanted much of his earlier philosophy and was suggesting a parenting approach that emphasized setting limits for children's behavior. For many parents, Dr. Spock's about-face was the first clue that the "experts" on child-rearing were fallible, too.

Pressure to Succeed

A countertrend in child-rearing, which held special appeal for ambitious upper-middle-class parents, was the push to turn ordinary kids into geniuses. In the 1970s, Glenn Doman's *How to Teach Your Baby to Read* made the bestseller list; soon moms and dads across the nation were making pilgrimages to Doman's "Better Baby Institute" in Philadelphia, and determinedly waving flash cards before the eyes of their puzzled toddlers. Parents in wealthy suburbs clamored for "gifted and talented" programs in the public schools. Private tutorial services that offered high school students intensive prepping for college entrance exams mushroomed into a multimillion-dollar industry.

Even as inner-city kids languished in crumbling, inadequate schools, those in the affluent suburbs tensed as their status-conscious parents stepped up the pressure for them to achieve and succeed in school. Many a bitter, desperate adolescent thought of ending his life after an academic setback—a poor grade on a report card, a rejection notice from his first-choice college—tarnished his sterling image and assaulted his sense of self-worth. This was just what happened to Jane, whose story appeared in Chapter One.

A few kernels of truth lay buried beneath all this folly: Ordinary children *are* capable of learning much more than they generally do, and good teaching *does* make a big difference. The trouble was that the quest for smarter kids was easily deformed into a status contest among highly competitive parents. In some cases, the motivating force was a parent's deep hunger for reflected glory, not the child's delight in academic achievement and mastery. A teen in this position lived in constant danger of losing parental approval, support, and even love if his grades and test scores didn't measure up to Mom and Dad's expectations.

Eddie's Story

Eddie, the only son of a wealthy, achievement-oriented professional couple, was a history major at a prestigious small college in the Northwest. For his senior thesis, Eddie decided to write a comprehensive history of Europe, even though his faculty adviser repeatedly warned him that this was an impossibly ambitious task in light of the time available. Sure enough, Eddie floundered, failed to complete the thesis by the due date, and did not graduate with the rest of his class.

The following September, Eddie was back at the college, living alone in an off-campus rented apartment and struggling with his monumental thesis project. Suffering from acute writer's block, he went for several months without accomplishing anything. One crisp, snowy morning in December, Eddie's girlfriend knocked on his door and got no answer. Opening the door, she stepped into the living room—and recoiled, screaming in pure terror. Eddie's inert body lay sprawled in an armchair, the head swollen beyond its normal size. The shotgun with which he had shot himself lay on the floor beside him. He had been dead for many hours.

In his suicide note, Eddie absolved his parents and friends of any responsibility for his death. "*Since I realize I will never accomplish anything worthwhile,*" he wrote, "*it is pointless for me to go on.*" He was 22 years old.

Moms On the Job

Yet another huge upheaval in the American family from the 1960s through the 1980s was the increasing number of mothers in the workforce. With the rising divorce rate, many newly single mothers took jobs out of simple economic necessity. Also, in the groundswell of feminism that gathered momentum in the late 1960s, many women—including mothers—began to claim their right to paid work and equal opportunity on the job.

By the 1980s, the U.S. economy had changed dramatically: There were fewer production jobs and many more low-paying jobs in the service sector, and the cost of housing in many areas had risen drastically. Two-parent families found it increasingly hard to make ends meet on the father's income alone. As the years passed and these trends continued, mothers with jobs became the rule rather than the exception. Most worked because they needed the money. But others worked because social expectations had changed; many an educated woman could not hold her head high if she had to admit she was "just a housewife and mother."

Child care, unfortunately, was slow to catch up. Even at the end of the 1980s, public schooling in most areas began only after a child's fifth birthday, and the school day ended in mid-afternoon while parents were still at work. Day-care centers were rare, expensive, and largely unregulated; reliable nannies were costly and hard to find. Mothers who worked were often forced to leave young children at home unattended for many hours, with only the TV for company. "Latchkey children" had long been a subject of national concern, yet the politically conservative administration passed no social legislation to alleviate the problem. Increasingly, unsupervised children and teenagers spent many hours of the day alone, at home or on the streets.

The woman who helped bring home the bacon was apt to claim her fair share of power in making family decisions. But in many cases, the husband, who had grown up thinking that men should call the shots, was ambivalent about sharing the role of breadwinner and head-of-family. The resulting resentments and arguments generated family tensions that helped contribute to the ever-rising divorce rate. Caught in the crossfire was the child: emotionally and/or physically neglected, upset and guilty about his parents' psychological warfare, isolated from grandparents and other relatives whose presence might have comforted him, lacking a religious or spiritual context to fall back on, and in some cases disoriented by the family's recent move to a new town or a fancier neighborhood. Adolescent alienation and resentment ballooned, and the teen suicide rate kept rising.

The Family in Disarray

In short, American family life after World War II deteriorated seriously, buffeted by the high winds of technological, economic, and social change. As we enter the 1990s, the profile of the typical family bears almost no resemblance to its postwar self:

- Grandparents, aunts, and uncles are absent from the hearth.
- The house itself may be just one in a long series of temporary residences.

- Chances are good that the parents have divorced, and that the child lives with a single mother or with a remarried mother or father.
- The child of divorce shuttles back and forth between her mother's and her father's homes, perhaps dealing with a parent and a stepparent in both places.
- The family is not "plugged into" its community: no church membership, no volunteer activities, no civic responsibilities beyond mandatory recycling.
- The mother works, and the child spends lonely hours at home alone after school each day.
- What Mom and Dad do at work is an abstraction. The child has no chance to *see* grownups at work and visualize his future self as a grownup in the workforce.

Thus, for many young people, the family is a far cry from that comforting, reassuring Norman Rockwell-style haven. Parents are harried, distracted, overworked, and absent much of the time. In addition, many of them are confused about what limits to set, what rules to enforce.

Emile Durkheim, the social theorist I mentioned in Chapter One, used the word *anomie* to describe a psychological sense of deadness and emptiness. Anomie is the soulless condition of societies in which important institutions, such as the family, have broken down so quickly that people no longer know what their attitudes and goals are or should be. According to Durkheim, suicide rates in anomic societies are considerably higher than in more rigid cultures, in which people clearly see their roles in life.

As home became a less and less cozy place, disoriented American teens felt increasingly cast adrift in a strange, unfriendly, anomic society—and their suicide rate rose relentlessly.

3

It's an Alienating World Out There

The family was not the only American institution to undergo radical change in the years between 1960 and 1990. Over the past 30 years, we have seen our social order realign itself over and over again.

New Gadgets, New Lifestyles

As each technological invention came along, whole portions of our way of life transformed to accommodate the new arrival. Often the result was greater isolation of people from one another. This was hard on everyone, of course. But it was particularly hard on teenagers, who, struggling with a changing body image and groping for a niche in life, needed plenty of warm human contact to help keep them on an even keel.

- In many households, *television* took the place of conversation. Some kids who grew up watching the tube ended up knowing TV characters better than they knew real people. With one or more TV sets in every house, siblings and friends did not necessarily even have the shared experience of watching the same shows together.

- With the advent of headphones and personal-size *cassette players,* people could listen to their choice of music or readings even while driving their car or jogging around the park. It was possible to spend much of the day in a personal electronic bubble, cut off from other people.
- *Computer* technology changed not only the workplace but also the home. Parents whose jobs involved many hours of silent tapping on a computer keyboard now came home to find their preteen and adolescent children, especially the boys, camped in front of the TV screen, mutely pushing the control buttons on a home video game.

What ever happened to those old-fashioned moments kids used to share with one another—summer days exploring the woods or the neighborhood, winter afternoons playing ice hockey or racing on the frozen pond, spring Saturdays absorbed in baseball or bike riding? Increasingly those times were giving way to endless hours of solitary electronic entertainment. People might romanticize the past to an extent, but their sense of something missing was real. Life for kids was becoming strangely two-dimensional. In a word, the new lifestyle was depressing. And as we know, isolation and depression are at the heart of many teenager suicide attempts.

Violence: A Staple Commodity

As movies and television continued to provide young people with images of what life outside the family looked like, the creators of these shows gave their viewers more and more of what they thought would excite and please: violence.

Why does violence take center stage in so much of our entertainment? We don't know all the answers, but one thing is certain: Although violence on the screen does not appeal to everyone, it's an extremely marketable commodity, particularly among adolescents. Producers make violent films because they know large numbers of people will watch them. Eventually viewers get used to a certain level of televised violence, and this ups the ante; in a spiral effect, producers turn out even more violent shows. Because television is only minimally regulated, kids are able from a young age to tune in regularly to shows that dramatize mortal threats, brutal beatings, shootings, stabbings, and murder in many forms. In addition, TV news is full of bombings, burnings, assassinations, and terrorist attacks that are all too real.

The end result is a culture that's rather blasé about violence. We in the United States see so much violence in the movies that scenes of war on the evening news move us only slightly, and accounts of brutal rapes and murders in our cities hardly touch us.

Thus, the adolescent who is considering suicide is no stranger to the trappings of violence. Death by gunshot wound, or by leaping off a high bridge, or by driving off a cliff, may even seem attractively "macho." In most cases, the young person has little or no personal experience of the ugliness and finality of death, which might serve to counteract these romantic notions.

Mixing It Up in the Melting Pot

It's a cliché, but still true, that the United States is a melting pot—or, more accurately, a patchwork quilt—of races and cultures. Since people are by nature somewhat xenophobic—that is, wary of those who are unlike themselves—our gloriously messy, increasingly heterogeneous American culture generates a lot of anxiety. Having to rub elbows with people of different colors and customs goes along with the American dream of a free and just society, but for many people it isn't at all easy.

Lingering racial and cultural prejudices and stereotypes maintain tensions in neighborhoods, in schools, and on the job.

With respect to African-Americans, race relations came a long way between 1960 and 1990. The Civil Rights Movement of the 1960s ended the Jim Crow laws and tacit segregation that had excluded black people from much of mainstream American life. In the following decades, stepped-up integration in the public schools helped overcome racial separatism, at least outwardly.

Yet many of today's black teenagers feel they are still far from parity with white teens. In some cases, attending a racially mixed school makes things worse. In an integrated setting, they confront not only prejudice from white youngsters, but also pressure from black kids who scorn "Oreos": kids perceived to be "black on the outside, white on the inside." Another stumbling block is some teachers' and administrators' (usually unacknowledged) assumption that black kids are low achievers, more interested in recreation than in academics.

White teens from certain ethnic backgrounds—Hispanic and, in some cases, Italian—also struggle with stereotypes that paint them as unintelligent and uninterested in school achievement. The stereotypes act as self-fulfilling prophecies: Kids who think they are destined to become dropouts do indeed tend to leave school before graduating.

Oriental Americans, who began entering the public schools in large numbers in the 1970s and 1980s, contend with a different set of problems. Pegged as brilliant superachievers, Asian kids struggle to live up to expectations that they will always excel. In school they must counteract resentment from youngsters of other races who see them as cutthroat academic rivals. At home, many are under great family pressure not to become Westernized. In urban school parlance, the Oriental counterpart to the "Oreo" is the "Twinkie": yellow outside, white inside.

For adolescents, then, racial and cultural tensions

serve to confuse life in a world already complicated by widespread family disintegration, increasing personal isolation, and an ethic of violence as glamour. Hopeless acceptance of a negative racial stereotype is a stress factor acknowledged by many teenagers who have contemplated or attempted suicide.

Women on the Move

Girls and women in the United States went through the wringer from the 1960s through the 1980s. Waves of feminism had rocked the country in times past—suffragists, for instance, finally won the vote for women in 1920—but the years immediately following World War II were a period of quiet retrenchment into traditional home-and-family values. Throughout the 1950s, the ideal held up to women was a life dedicated to husband and four-or-so children.

In 1963, Betty Friedan's *The Feminine Mystique,* the manifesto of the bored housewife, hit the bestseller list. Suddenly, middle-class women realized that they were spending much of their lives repressing anger and resentment at society's artificial constraints on their lives. What good was their precious schooling, if the only job that afforded them any security and prestige was wife-mother-homemaker? Gradually it began to seem acceptable, at least in theory, for a woman to combine child-rearing and a career, or even to skip motherhood altogether.

Women dove into the Civil Rights Movement, but often found themselves relegated to making coffee for the men. They plunged into the counterculture, but discovered that "male chauvinism" was a trait that bearded hippies and smooth-shaven straights had in common. As the economy tightened after the U.S. military pulled out of Vietnam, and families struggled to make ends meet, women rushed to take jobs that promised financial security—only to find themselves stuck in the pink-collar ghetto.

The 1980s were a decade of grim corporate gamesmanship, with women determined to break the "old boy" network and climb the ranks of management. Betty Lehan Harrigan's *Games Mother Never Taught You* showed women how to dress for success and talk about business using football metaphors. Manufacturers of everything from clothes to bathroom fixtures churned out upscale product lines aimed at the new Yuppie trendsetters, half of whom were women.

As the 1980s melted into the 1990s, women who had "made it" in the business or professional world were rethinking their priorities. Many who finally interrupted their careers to have children were appalled, upon returning to work, at the lack of decent, affordable child care. Reluctant to sacrifice their children to their careers, they pressured employers for new rights: flexible hours including work time at home, job-sharing possibilities, paternity leave for new fathers, subsidized day care. Corporations, dismayed at the potential cost of these new benefits, resisted.

Gender Role Confusion

During these decades of change, girls growing into womanhood were both excited and intimidated by the new possibilities opening up to them. As schools gradually moved to give girls and boys truly equal opportunity in math and the sciences, adolescent girls saw the future as a wide horizon. For most of their mothers, career choices had been limited to teaching and nursing, with motherhood calling a halt to all professional activity. Now, the sky seemed the limit.

In addition, advances in contraception allowed many women a new degree of freedom to be sexually active. The old double standard—virginity for unmarried women, "experience" for unmarried men—seemed on its way out. The Supreme Court's 1972 *Roe v. Wade* decision, which legalized abortion, boosted women's sense of control over their destiny.

Girls' new confidence, however, was sometimes more apparent than real. Their role models were limited, since they still saw relatively few women in prestigious, well-paid jobs. Did a woman really have what it took to become a doctor, a metallurgist, a systems analyst? Studies in the 1980s documented young women's "fear of success"—their tendency to drop out just before or just after reaching an academic or career goal. Behind this failure of nerve was uncertainty about a woman's "true place" in life. If she pursued a career, would she never be a mommy? If she earned an impressive salary, would guys be turned off? And was she really at liberty to express herself sexually, or was she in danger, after all, of developing a bad reputation?

Boys weren't sure how to react to feminism. Most felt vaguely that it was only decent to support full job equality for women. But did that mean boys should no longer pay for the movies? Did it mean men shouldn't open car doors for women? Should a fellow break up with a woman who wasn't sexually faithful to him? If a guy married a feminist, would he end up as a "househusband" whose wife paid the bills and made the decisions? Most adolescent boys and young men were intimidated by the evolution of gender roles through these three decades. A guy was no longer sure what he was supposed to do—or what *she* was supposed to do.

Gay and lesbian rights movements allowed many homosexual people to come out of the closet. Homosexuality, formerly deeply taboo, gradually earned a measure of acceptance in the more liberal segments of American society. Yet fear of homosexuality was still widespread: Military recruiters routinely rejected gay men; lesbian women who got divorced saw their ex-husbands gain custody of their children. The teenager who felt same-sex attractions was torn between a desire for honesty and a need to survive in a hypocritical, homophobic world.

Gender role confusion in these three decades made adolescence and young adulthood more difficult than ever before. With the relationship between the sexes no longer clearly defined, forging a satisfactory personal identity often seemed an impossible task. Some young people were so unsure of what was expected of them that they simply avoided the opposite sex. Others who entered relationships were depressed and discouraged by the constant struggle to guard against, combat, or atone for "sexist" behavior.

As the AIDS epidemic surfaced in the 1980s, the initial reaction—a backlash against homosexuals—transformed into a haunted quest for safe sex for everyone. Was the "sexual revolution" over? Once again, the rules of the game had changed.

With gender roles in a state of flux, many teens and young adults despaired of ever "finding themselves" or achieving intimacy with anyone. The resulting isolation was one more stress factor nudging vulnerable adolescents toward suicidal behavior.

Nuclear Nightmares

From the 1960s onward, kids had to come to terms with a threat unknown in their parents' and grandparents' youth: the sinister possibility that nuclear war would wipe the human race off the face of the earth.

Although some experts make light of the nuclear threat as an influence on teenagers' personal philosophy, I believe the specter of nuclear holocaust is a significant stressor for thoughtful adolescents everywhere. Acknowledging the possibility of nuclear attack means facing the fact that one vengeful impulse by a power-crazed politician, or even one misinterpretation of computerized military data, could put an instant end to life as we know it. In past ages, when people fantasized about the end of the world, they imagined it as an act of God. Today, we know that the real danger of Armageddon lies in the mismanagement of *human* capabilities.

I think the philosophical net result has been an overall devaluation of life. If one lunatic can destroy us all with the push of a button, what's the use in getting involved with people and projects and goals? This is the conclusion many intelligent teenagers reach when they first realize the full scope of the nuclear threat.

Most young people gradually accommodate to the nuclear nightmare as they continue to live, mature, and form attachments to other people. Although awareness of the possibility of nuclear disaster never really disappears, it eventually takes up residence in an obscure corner of the mind.

But kids who are still adjusting to the prospect of nuclear annihilation search their minds for possible ways to escape the horror of surviving atomic warfare. Suicide occurs to them as a natural route of escape. Those Brown University students I mentioned in Chapter One—the ones who wanted the school infirmary to keep cyanide capsules on hand so they could choose suicide in the event of nuclear war—are a good example. In response to their very real fears of overwhelming horror, they made a collective decision that suicide was a legitimate way they could assert some control over their destiny.

The Terrible Triad: Cars, Guns, and Drugs

Adding to the dangers surrounding teenagers in the past three decades was the easy availability of what mental health professionals call the terrible triad: cars, guns, and drugs.

Cars

Learning to drive is almost every teenager's dream, and once that precious license is acquired the next step is getting access to a car. Beginning in the 1960s, the sons and daughters of the comfortably well-off got new cars as birthday and graduation presents. Those of the struggling middle class worked and saved to buy used cars. Poor kids did without—but were sometimes tempted to steal a car for a few minutes or hours of freedom.

Automobile insurance companies know the score, but most parents have only a vague idea of the danger to society posed by an out-of-control youngster, especially a young man, at the wheel of a car. Psychiatrist Derek Miller writes, with typical understatement: "A false sense of personal power is given to adolescents who are allowed to drive automobiles at the age of sixteen, when they may find it difficult to place the boundaries of the automobile in space." A growing boy, who has not even developed a reliable mental image of his own body, is easily confused about how much space a car occupies and what will happen when he drives aggressively. This helps to explain the extraordinarily high number of auto-related adolescent deaths, many of which are unrecognized suicides. A depressed or angry teen, in an instant of impulsiveness, floors the gas pedal and steers toward a wall or an embankment—and the result is a suicide that looks like an accident.

According to forensic experts and highway safety officials, auto fatalities account for some 37 percent of all deaths of youngsters aged 15 to 24, and about one-fourth of the "accidents" are actually deliberate. Adding these so-called autocides to known suicide statistics would raise suicide to the number-one killer in this age group.

Guns

Firearms used to be utilitarian items mainly kept

for hunting, or collector's items to be displayed behind glass doors. But with the urbanization of American society and the ever-increasing level of violence in the cities, many people began to feel that owning and carrying a gun was simply reasonable self-protective behavior.

By the 1980s, formerly peaceful neighborhoods in various cities throughout the country had become virtual war zones as drug-dealing gangs, playing for incredibly high stakes, used semi-automatic weapons against police officers and rival dealers. More and more children and teenagers saw guns at home, knew where they were kept, and understood how they worked.

Adolescent boys, in particular, gravitate toward guns as a means of suicide: The suddenness, the drama, the violence of death by gunshot wins their admiration because it embellishes the stereotype of manliness. The sheer availability of firearms over the past three decades has ensured a growing number of teenager suicides-by-gunshot.

Drugs

Teenage alcohol and drug use, which climbed inexorably from the turned-on hippie era of the mid-1960s through the late 1980s, made access to guns and cars infinitely more deadly. Alcohol, which was and still is America's drug of choice, impairs both reflexes and judgment. Marijuana, an insidiously alienating drug which enjoyed enormous popularity from the 1960s onward, does the same. LSD and the other psychedelics cause hallucinations; cocaine and amphetamines release a rush of barely controllable energy, excitement, and impatience.

The kid who is high on alcohol or drugs is more apt to drive recklessly, take foolish chances, use a gun impulsively, and not care about the consequences. The teen who is hopelessly mired in alcohol or drug dependency is sometimes depressed and hopeless enough to consider suicide, either by car "accident" or by gunshot, as a way out of life's misery. Even a teen who's not in chronic trouble with drugs might get high at a party, temporarily experience an altered sense of reality, and entertain thoughts of suicide.

An Unfriendly World

The deliberately grim picture I have painted in this chapter highlights the strains and tears in the American social fabric from the 1960s through the 1980s. On adults, these stresses are hard enough; on kids, they sometimes prove fatal.

The teen who feels at odds with everyone and everything is surrounded by plenty of evidence that the world is a confusing, unfriendly, alienating place.

Since many adults, including parents, are too preoccupied or troubled to provide effective guidance, some teens have been left to find their own solutions to the classic adolescent problems of loneliness, anxiety, shifting identity, and the search for autonomy. Alienation has been their primary problem.

With social and cultural norms changing so quickly, other teens, the sons and daughters of immigrants, have found themselves caught in a time warp: yearning to join the alluring mainstream culture, but thwarted by strict parents who set archaic standards of behavior. Frustration is their biggest problem.

Added to the basic teen problems of alienation, frustration, and the hovering possibility of nuclear destruction are the peculiar stresses of modern American life—ubiquitous violence presented as entertainment, complicated social tensions among rival racial and ethnic groups, prolonged uncertainty over gender roles, easy and unsupervised access to cars, and the appalling availability of alcohol, drugs, and guns. For adolescents, this heady combination of social forces has translated into three decades of uncertainty, discomfort, and ultimately, rising suicide rates.

But social causes of adolescent suicide, although important and often overlooked, are only part of the story. In the next three chapters of this book, I'll approach the subject from other perspectives. Let's move on to explore adolescent psychological processes and examine some of the thoughts that run through the minds of teens and young adults who are contemplating suicide.

PART TWO

INSIDE THE MIND OF A SUICIDAL TEEN

4

The Last Straw

Now that we have seen how social forces can work inexorably to boost the adolescent suicide rate, it's time to shift gears and take a look at the thought processes of kids who try to end their lives.

Anyone who attempts suicide is reaching for an ultimate, dramatic solution to life's problems. But since teenagers have their whole lives ahead of them, how serious can their problems really be?

The answer is: quite serious, at least to them. In the most common suicide scenario, a kid has been coping poorly with several difficulties for some time. Then one more thing goes wrong, and suicide starts to look like an answer.

The last straw, usually a loss or setback, might be any one of these:

- A death or divorce in the family
- A breakup with a boyfriend or girlfriend
- A move to a new school
- Failing to make the team
- Giving up the winning run
- Getting pregnant
- Having a huge argument with a parent

It's not that any of these events by itself is enough to drive a teenager to commit suicide. But for a youngster whose prevailing mood is one of alienation, depression, or deep frustration, a single adverse event can suddenly take on unusual importance, as if it were a metaphor for the kids' whole life. The kid who sees this new problem as the final, unbearable insult thinks: *Why keep on living, if this is what life is all about?*

Moving from Thought to Action

Perhaps the youngster has already toyed with the idea of suicide once or many times. This is not at all unusual: 24 percent of people in general, and 32 percent of college students, admit to having *thought* of suicide at some point in their lives. But thought, according to psychiatrist Leo Rangell, is nothing more than trial action: the way the mind "sees" different versions of what is, was, or might be. Thus, a suicidal thought is not as serious an occurrence as a suicidal *wish*.

And a suicidal wish is not as serious as a *plan* to commit suicide. The kid who actually works out the details of how to commit suicide has moved one step further away from the possibility of a "life" solution and toward the possibility of a "death" solution.

A suicide plan, although serious business, is not yet a suicide *attempt*. The young person may work out the most minute details of the suicide, and even write the suicide note, load the gun, or climb the bridge—but still back down at the critical moment. One 20-year-old woman recalled, "I got everything ready and I lay down and put the plastic bag over my head, but I couldn't go through with it. I was thinking about how they would feel when they found me, and I suddenly realized what a horrible, horrible thing I would be doing to them."

Likewise, a suicide attempt does not necessarily produce suicide. As we saw in Chapter One, only a fraction of all suicide attempts actually result in death. Often the youngster leaves a large loophole in what is otherwise an efficient death plan: takes the phone off the hook, unlocks the apartment door, swallows too few pills.

Eerily, a spark of the will to live may flare up brightly even after the youngster has dived off the cliff or pulled the trigger. Rangell quotes one of the rare jumpers who survived his leap off the Golden Gate Bridge: "From the instant I saw my hand leave the railing, I knew I wanted to live. I was terrified out of my skull."

The Balance of Forces

In an everyday setting, motivation for wanting to live—whether for adolescents or older people—boils down to a few simple factors:

- Satisfaction, rather than frustration
- A sense of self-worth, rather than worthlessness
- Hope, rather than despair
- Control, rather than helplessness
- A clear conscience, rather than guilt

Naturally, it's a matter of ups and downs, of balance between these opposing forces—there's probably something wrong with the person who always feels totally satisfied, hopeful, in control, and guiltless! My point is this: if a kid finds himself on the downside in most or all of these reason-to-live categories, even an apparently trivial setback can turn into a last-straw experience—a nudge toward suicide.

Which circumstances are likely to tip an adolescent toward the negative, life-denying side of the scale? One heartrending scenario, all too familiar to mental health professionals, involves the "throwaway kid": the adolescent who has ample reason to believe that no one cares about him.

Opposing Forces: What Makes a Teenager Want to Live or Die?

Emotional balance is precarious in the teen years. When a youngster's reasons to die outweigh reasons to live, the stage is set for a suicide attempt.

REASONS TO LIVE		REASONS TO DIE
Satisfaction	←→	Frustration
Sense of self-worth	←→	Worthlessness
Hope	←→	Despair
Control	←→	Helplessness
Clear conscience	←→	Guilt

Michael: A Throwaway Kid

In *The Cop and the Kid,* a real-life account by William Fox with Noel Hynd, 17-year-old Michael climbed to the top of a tall building in New York City intending to jump, but police were able to rescue him. He told social workers his story.

Born in the South to a mother who abandoned him, Michael lived until the age of eight with his father's parents, who treated him well. But when both grandparents died and his alcoholic father deserted, he was placed in a foster home. The foster family took steps to adopt Michael, but then backed out of the adoption and moved to another part of the country, leaving him behind.

Michael fell into the abyss of the child welfare system. In the following years he lurched from one miserable placement to the next: a state home where older boys beat him up and sodomized him, unsatisfactory foster homes, youth centers meant for dangerous delinquents. After stealing a car and doing time in jail, he broke parole and fled to New York.

Life on the city streets was much rougher than he had ever imagined. After a few weeks of sleeping on park benches and in subway cars, Michael found a menial job and took a room in a reeking flophouse. Suddenly, looking at the drunken derelicts dozing in the lobby, he had a horrifying revelation: He had sunk to the level of the bums. Like them, and like his father, he had no family, no home, no education. He was alone in the world, and his prospects for the future were miserable.

Michael spent the night sobbing. The next day he made his way to the top of the building, inched onto a narrow ledge, and stared down at the sidewalk six floors below. Callous onlookers shouted, "Jump! Jump!" Michael was still weeping helplessly when the police rescue team arrived and gently talked him out of making the fatal leap.

Michael's perceptions were accurate: He *was* alone in the world, abandoned and helpless. He spent several more months wasting away inside the New York social welfare system, and he made another suicide attempt—this time by slashing his wrists. But then his life took a miraculous turn for the better. One of the police officers who had rescued him from the rooftop legally adopted him, and Michael reaped the psychological benefits of real parenting for the first time in eleven years.

Understanding Michael

You may recall the five common themes of adolescent suicide that I mentioned in Chapter One: self-murder, retaliatory abandonment, control over the death process, reunion, and rebirth. In Michael's case, the major theme was self-murder. Because neglect and emotional deprivation had been the norm throughout his whole young life, he had an extremely low opinion of himself: No one loved him, so he assumed he was unlovable.

Thus, low self-worth was Michael's background condition. Running away to New York City added to the stress in his life, since the city proved dangerous and cold. The last straw was the moment when, having paid in advance for his room, he suddenly looked around at the drunken bums in the filthy flophouse and realized that he had joined their ranks. His worst fears about himself seemed to be confirmed. He lost all hope.

Michael was what some social workers call a "throwaway kid": a child whose parents had discarded him as though he were a disposable object. Unfortunately, the only thing unusual about his story is its upbeat ending. City shelters are full of teenage runaways who have fled families unwilling to care for them. Despite the conscientious work of the shelters, many of these castoff adolescents succumb to drug addiction, prostitution, AIDS—and suicide.

When parents consciously or unconsciously wish their child were dead or had never been born, the child is likely to understand and internalize their attitude and to "grow up dead"—convinced that he has no real right to live. (It's sad to note than even when a "throwaway kid" finds a loving home, the deep emotional wounds of the past may not heal over and disappear. Sometimes a seemingly minor incident ignites a fire of resentment and self-hatred that leads to a suicidal act.)

Colleen: Dirty Little Secrets

Another unfortunately common scenario involves the sexually abused child. Pert, red-haired, green-eyed Colleen had problems entirely different from Michael's. Her parents cared for her and paid attention to her. In fact, her handsome, witty father often gave her too much attention—of the wrong kind.

When she was a little girl and the two of them were alone in the house, he would play a game with her:

stroking and tickling her body, and inevitably her crotch, to make her laugh. As time passed, the game got more elaborate. Daddy showed her that she could take her panties off "to make it tickle more." He taught her to unzip his jeans and feel inside his undershorts, but he warned her never to tell Mommy. "You're my special little girl," he told her. "This is our secret."

Although Colleen did feel special and coyly kept their secret for years, the games had come to seem vaguely sinister by the time she reached puberty. Daddy had taught her what he liked her to do with her hands and mouth, but she was disturbed by the way it made him act. Lately he was always eager to explore inside her vagina, which she tolerated uneasily.

One evening when Mommy was out bowling, Daddy coaxed 13-year-old Colleen into bed and then had intercourse with her. "You're so beautiful, baby," he whispered. "You're Daddy's secret angel." But Colleen didn't feel beautiful. What he was doing to her was painful, and she suddenly had the strong conviction that it was very wrong. She felt angry and ashamed, and she resolved to tell her mother.

Mommy did seem outraged at what Colleen told her, but also ashamed and frightened. Her reply to Colleen sounded like a jumble of nonsense: "I'm sure that can't be exactly what happened. Your father wouldn't do that. Aren't you exaggerating a little? He was probably just playing, and you're trying to make it into a big problem. Anyway, you know how he is—he never could hold his liquor. Just don't say anything to anyone." Baffled, resentful, and scared, Colleen decided she hated her mother. In subsequent months the two of them fought constantly. She tried to avoid her father, but sometimes he managed to get her alone. When she resisted his advances, he soothed and flattered her until she gave in.

At age 14, Colleen went on a date with a 19-year-old who took her to the movies and then forced sex on her in the back seat of his car. She wanted to kill him. When she got home that night her mother had gone to bed, but her father, who was waiting up for her, put his arms around her and gently pulled her down onto the couch. Furiously she broke away, dashed into her room, and locked the door. She didn't sleep at all, but spent the night grimly cleaning and tidying her room.

The next morning after her parents left for work, Colleen took a razor blade, sat down on the edge of the bathtub, and made deep cuts in both of her wrists. The once-a-week cleaning woman arrived ten minutes later, found her weeping and bleeding in the bathroom, and called the rescue squad. Colleen survived and was referred for psychiatric treatment.

Understanding Colleen

The predominant psychological theme of Colleen's suicide attempt was retaliatory abandonment. Even though her parents had always taken good care of her physically, she felt emotionally abandoned by both of them. Her father told her that he loved and cherished her, and perhaps he did. However, he was exploiting her, using her selfishly for his own sexual gratification—something it took her years to understand. Colleen's mother abandoned her emotionally by failing to respond to her plea for protection against the father's sexual advances.

Thus, shame, confusion, and emotional abandonment were Colleen's background state. The shock, anger, and humiliation of the date rape, immediately followed by her father's thoughtless sexual come-on in the living room, added up to the last straw. Colleen suddenly saw herself as faceless, powerless, and passive: the quintessential sex object, existing only to be used. Seeing no other way to strike back, she resolved to commit suicide.

You may find it incredible that Colleen's mother took no action when Colleen "told on" her father, but this is a rather typical feature of incest dynamics. In family therapy, it became clear that Colleen's mother had been intuitively aware of the father-daughter intimacy for many years. However, she was sure her husband would leave her if she showed the slightest suspicion or jealousy. Since she was terrified of abandonment, she suppressed the incriminating thoughts. When Colleen finally appealed for help, the mother was literally unable to understand or respond to her daughter's plea. Of course, Colleen assumed this meant her mother didn't care.

Many sexually abused teenage children are extraordinarily ambivalent toward the adult who molests them. In the end, Colleen feared and resented her father's insistent sexual overtures. But for many years there was a part of her that enjoyed the attention, and the knowledge that in his eyes she was the most special female in the world.

Erin: Lipstick, Dancing, and Dishonor

Little Erin, a bright, energetic, and obedient young child, was a delight to both her parents. They were simple, earnest people who belonged to a very strict fundamentalist church, and they brought up their daughter according to a rigid moral code.

Storm clouds appeared over this picture of domestic harmony when blonde, willowy Erin reached puberty. At age 13, surrounded by school friends who enjoyed a great deal of personal liberty, she began complaining to her parents that she wanted "more of a social life." When they asked what she meant, she mentioned things like using makeup and going to school dances. Absolutely not, they said.

One day when she was 14, Erin, driven by curiosity, defied her parents by putting on lipstick. Their reaction was swift and unequivocal: they beat her severely with a switch and restricted her to the house for two weeks.

About a month later, even though she was well

aware that her parents meant business, Erin defied them again. She came home one evening at 9:00 and admitted to them that she had briefly gone to a school dance, "just to see what it was like." This time, their reaction was catastrophic. Since she had proved incorrigible by their standards, they formally disowned her in the old-fashioned way. In their house, they told her, she would still have food and a place to sleep—but nothing more. From that moment on they refused to speak to her, treating her as though she were invisible. They took the necessary steps to get her excommunicated from the church.

Over the next month, emotionally cut off from her parents and from the religious community in which she had grown up, Erin seemed to waste away. She ate and slept very little and went through school each day in a daze; her grades dropped and she shrank from any social contact. Because she was so obviously troubled, and because her parents refused to meet with any teachers, counselors, and administrators, a school psychologist referred her for an evaluation. The psychiatrist who saw her noted that her depression was among the most profound he had ever seen. He immediately admitted her to the hospital's adolescent unit. Even after several weeks of antidepressant medication and intensive counseling, however, Erin remained extremely depressed.

One day, tragedy struck. Erin was one of a group of adolescents who attended a group therapy session in an office near the hospital unit. The patients, ever curious and out of immediate sight of the staff group leader, suddenly discovered something interesting inside a desk drawer: a large sample of antidepressant pills, probably left there by a salesman. Erin quickly grabbed the pills and stuck them in her purse. The kids who saw her take the pills treated it as a joke; they said nothing to the therapist or the other group members. Shortly thereafter, Erin asked to go to the ladies' room; it must have been there that she swallowed all 100 pills. Back at the hospital, several hours later, friends found her passed out on her bed. Erin never awakened from her coma. Despite intensive emergency treatment, she died that evening.

Understanding Erin

If you think Erin's is a rather unusual example of a home situation that led to a teenage suicide, you're right: Relatively few parents are this extreme in their religious and moral convictions. Yet I include Erin's story here because her suicide was such a clear-cut and dramatic example of suicide as retaliatory abandonment.

Like Colleen, Erin had enjoyed years of happiness and closeness with her parents. Unlike Colleen, however, she suffered a sudden, total loss of emotional support when her parents disowned her. In committing suicide, she expressed her absolute rage—at her parents and probably also at the church community—over their total emotional abandonment of her.

Erin was overwhelmed with grief at being left emotionally out in the cold. At the same time, she was furious at her own powerlessness to change the situation. When she got the unexpected opportunity to swallow an overdose of pills, she did so without hesitation. Her crushing grief and helpless rage, a powerful combination, made her reckless: If everyone who was important in her life could ruthlessly abandon her, then she would ruthlessly abandon them in return. Suicide was the way she chose to do it.

Jerry: Cruelty and Control

Jerry's childhood was fairly uneventful until, when he was about five years old, his divorced mother remarried. Her new husband, a tough, hard-drinking police officer, disliked Jerry and beat him severely whenever he stepped out of line—which seemed to be all the time. Whether Jerry spilled a glass of milk, got his shoes wet in the rain, or forgot his jacket at a friend's house, his stepfather would find a pretext for harsh criticism and a violent thrashing with a thick leather belt.

Jerry's mother, an unpredictable woman who periodically tried to "get strict" with her son, was eventually diagnosed as having manic-depressive disorder. During her first dramatic manic episode, which occurred when Jerry was six years old, she flew into a rage and very nearly strangled him to death.

Jerry never did well in school. His aggressive cruelty towards girls got him into serious trouble, and he had ongoing truancy and behavior problems. By the time he was 15, his mother and stepfather admitted they were unable to handle him; at a doctor's suggestion, they sent him to live with his mother's parents for a year. Jerry "did okay" under the grandparents care, and returned to live with his parents the next year.

Back home that autumn, Jerry went to school fairly regularly and even made the football team. Problems started, however, when he began to get intimate with Kelly, a 33-year-old woman in a neighboring apartment who turned him on to "speed" (crystal methamphetamine), a drug in some ways similar to cocaine. High on speed much of the time, he began skipping school again. The football coach soon kicked him off the team, and the principal threatened him with expulsion.

Jerry's relationship with Kelly got stormy: he wanted her all to himself, but she persisted in seeing other men and said he had no business trying to restrict her. One Saturday night, during a heated argument, Kelly told Jerry it was all over between them. In front of her, Jerry swallowed and snorted a very large amount of speed. Then he staggered home, went into convulsions, and lost consciousness. Terrified, his parents brought him to a hospital emergency room. I met him a few days later, and admitted him to Southwood Hospital's adolescent unit.

Understanding Jerry

For Jerry, the major issue in life was control. Threatened and abused during his childhood by a heartless stepfather and an inconsistent, volatile mother, he felt a deep urge to call all the shots and to push other people around.

One way he coped was to lash out. When he was a young teenager, girls were his favorite targets because they were easy to intimidate. Another way he gained control was to thumb his nose at school. Being at large when other kids were cooped up in the classroom made him feel superior. Ridiculing the teachers was gratifying, because he knew they had little power to make him behave. When he got older, possessiveness with girlfriends was also a way Jerry exerted his control; he threatened to blacken the eye of any girl who two-timed him. Kelly was the first female who had ever stood up to him. Against the background of his failures at school and in football, her decision to break up with him was the last straw.

Serious drug abuse had been yet another coping mechanism for Jerry. Initially amphetamines energized him, replacing his deep self-doubts with feelings of power and super-competence. Later, the "crashes" that followed his euphorias wiped him out, robbing him of energy and initiative and sending him into crushing, black depressions. When Jerry failed to frighten Kelly into being faithful to him, he tried manipulation, overdosing right before her eyes to make her feel guilty about breaking up with him. (Drugs play a role in many suicides and suicide attempts, both because they can kill and because they encourage impulsivity. I'll go into this in more detail in Chapter Six.)

Jerry was given a dual diagnosis: suicidal depression plus dependency on drugs. At Southwood, his treatment dealt with both problems. The first task was to get him off drugs and teach him non-drug ways to cope with stress. The second was to treat his depressions and periodic rages.

Jerry had a long record of disruptive behavior, and his mother was manic-depressive. In light of this history, I decided to try him on lithium, a mood-stabilizing medication, once the illegal drugs were gone from his system. Lithium treatment made a big difference in Jerry's outlook on life. He gradually lost his mean streak, and started to take a genuine interest in "getting his act together." In therapy, Jerry decided he preferred living at his grandparents' house, and fortunately his family agreed to this plan. He stayed with his grandparents while finishing high school, became apprenticed to a welder, and eventually got his own apartment. So far he has managed to stay away from speed. He seems to have turned his life around.

Sandra: Trying to Turn the Clock Back

In early childhood Sandra was the classic "good girl," obedient and eager to please. As she reached puberty she began to feel ill at ease in the strict fundamentalist church to which her family belonged. However, throughout her teens she continued to attend Sunday and midweek services with her parents.

By her senior year of high school she had a boyfriend, Wayne, who attended the same church. Wayne, who was several years older than Sandra and worked for a large auto dealership, was ready to settle down. He asked Sandra to be his wife. Both families approved the match.

Although she felt she was deeply in love with Wayne, Sandra was not yet ready for marriage. An excellent student with strong artistic talent, she had won a generous scholarship to a college in a town several hundred miles away. She set off for college at age 18, asking Wayne to wait for her.

Living at college, Sandra was free for the first time to rebel from her strict upbringing. She remained a conscientious student, but she bleached her hair blond, wore trendy clothes, experimented with beer and marijuana, drew comic illustrations for the radical campus newspaper, and did not go to church the whole year. Through her newspaper activities she met David, a young philosophy major and avowed atheist who wrote political editorials. Before she knew it, she and David were involved in an intimate relationship.

Home for the summer after her freshman year, Sandra was preoccupied with thoughts of David. Wayne, who had been waiting faithfully for her, was openly delighted to have her back. She thought she still loved him, but she felt terribly guilty over her sexual adventure with David. She felt like an emotional yo-yo, one minute enjoying Wayne's lavish attentions, the next minute resenting him and secretly daydreaming that she was back at school with David. Church now seemed hollow and hypocritical to her, and she refused to attend services; this surprised her family and provoked heated arguments with her parents.

Suddenly, in August, disaster: Wayne was killed in a gruesome highway accident. Sandra was overcome by grief, remorse, and guilt. Had Wayne sensed her secret betrayal, and had that somehow caused his death? When she returned to college in September, she intended to pour out her heart to David. But David was strangely distant, and it didn't take Sandra long to find out why: He had a new girlfriend.

Over and over again, it occurred to her that she could set things right by rejoining Wayne in death. A few weeks into the semester, she swallowed an entire bottle of extra-strength aspirin, leaving a note to her family that said:

Wayne and I were meant to be. I can't go on without him. God meant for us to be together. I know you will understand.

She was rescued by a dormmate, who found her comatose and called the campus police.

Understanding Sandra

Sandra's attempted suicide showed her wish for a *reunion* with Wayne. Since early adolescence, she had been tempted to pull away from her rather straight-laced family. But in college, when she did dare to express some independence, she experienced guilt as well as exhilaration. Back home, she felt alienated from her family members, who were upset because she seemed to be rejecting the church. Her guilt deepened as her feelings toward Wayne became ambivalent. After he was killed, her burden of guilt was crushing.

When Sandra, grief-stricken and disoriented, went back to college and discovered David had found someone else, this betrayal was the last straw. She felt her life had taken a wrong turn down a blind alley. Suicide was her desperate attempt to undo past sins. She wanted to set the clock back and return to a time when life had been simpler and less confusing.

In therapy, as Sandra worked through her grief, she remembered that her relationship with Wayne had been partly unsatisfactory. Recognizing this came as a great relief to her, and helped her resolve some of her emotional confusion.

I mentioned in Chapter Two that shared religious values help give families a sense of cohesion. However, the adolescent child of a family that adheres rigidly to its faith sometimes feels a strong need to rebel, as Sandra did. Such youngsters often develop a deep religious faith later in life, although their chosen religion may not be the same as their parents'.

Importance of a Sympathetic Ear

As you have seen in the histories of Michael, Colleen, Erin, Jerry, and Sandra, a youngster can live with background unhappiness for months, or even many years, and not think seriously of suicide. Then a last-straw incident occurs, and the balance shifts. Reasons to live seem to be outweighed by reasons to die. For some kids, suicide suddenly begins to look like the only logical option.

At times like these, talking out the problems is the best way to defuse that suicidal impulse. An understanding grownup with a fresh perspective can help the youngster figure out different coping strategies and face life with renewed hope. But if no one recognizes the problem, offers a sympathetic ear, and reached out to help, then the kid may develop emotional "tunnel vision," getting more and more caught up in suicidal thoughts and plans.

Other Perspectives

Does this imply that all kids who commit suicide, or try to, are victims of profoundly unhappy life situations? No, certainly not all. Biological depression, certain physical conditions that affect the emotions, alcohol or drug abuse—any of these can underlie or provoke depressive states and trigger suicidal impulses. Before discussing physical and drug problems, however, I'd like to move into an exploration of the suicidal youngster's ruminations.

When a kid thinks of suicide, part of what goes through his mind are the imagined reactions of his family and friends: What will they say? How will they feel? What will they do? In the next chapter, let's see what these projections and fantasies can teach us.

5

"They'll Be Sorry When I'm Gone"

Suicide Notes

When a kid commits suicide or tries to, the horribly traumatized parents and siblings usually blame themselves—or one another. Was this in fact what the child intended? In other words, is suicide a young person's ultimate aggressive weapon against people he thinks treat him badly?

Admittedly, that's one possibility; "revenge" suicides do happen. However, it may be that the suicidal youngster had something entirely different in mind. If his suicide attempt does prove fatal, we can only speculate about his motivations—unless he is among the 10 percent to 35 percent who leave a suicide note behind.

A suicide note, which is basically a good-bye, is usually laced with hints of the emotional theme underlying the young person's suicide. Clues to his state of mind may be either spelled out or buried between the lines.

Strangely, the young person who writes a suicide note may assume that his family knows the reason for his suicide, so that an explanation is really unnecessary. It's as if the youngster felt he and the rest of the family had somehow merged identities, so that they could read his mind and know exactly what he was feeling.

The length of suicide notes varies tremendously. Some are short and direct. Others, especially those written by bright, articulate kids, can be long compositions, virtual autobiographies that include elaborate discussion of unsatisfactory relationships. Some notes give very detailed instructions to be carried out after the youngster's death.

Apologies

Perhaps the most pathetic of all suicide notes are those that convey the message, "You'll be better off without me." The kid who writes this kind of note has been so wounded by criticism that he has internalized it. Other people seem to find him a burden, and he thinks that's what he is. His self-esteem is so abysmally low that he actually believes the world will be a better, happier place without him.

Charles, who hanged himself in the bathroom at age 17, wrote:

> *This is for the best. At least I won't be around to bother you any more.*

From the age of six, Charles had been severely beaten by his father. His mother, who suffered from chronic depression, once tried to smother him with a pillow. Charles's school career was an endless string of behavior problems. He told a school counselor that he had daydreams about being dead, looking down on his parents and sister as they ate; they were talking together peacefully and seemed relieved that he was gone.

Thoughts of Reunion

After someone who was close to her dies, a youngster may be so overwhelmed by her loss that she feels she can't go on living. Suicide occurs to her as a way to rejoin the dead person. Iris, a painfully shy girl who was distraught at the death of her beloved grandmother, swallowed pills in an unsuccessful attempt to end her life. Before taking the pills, she wrote a note to her parents. It said:

> *I love you both, but I have to go and be with Grandma. I'm sure you'll understand.*

She obviously thought her parents were mind-readers who knew and understood her every thought.

In therapy, we discovered that Iris felt very guilty about her grandmother's death; she had failed to pay her usual visit one day, and the following day the elderly woman had passed away peacefully in her sleep. Iris feared that hurt and disappointment were what made her grandmother die.

Painful Losses

In a similar vein, a note sometimes refers to a recent emotional loss—not death, but a loss of love or closeness—as the motive for suicide. The youngster feels that the loss has caused her identity to collapse. Since she no longer has a sense of herself, she feels that in one way she is already dead. Suicide will merely complete the process.

Fran, who also took pills in an attempted suicide, was distraught because her boyfriend had left her. She wrote:

> *If I can't have Ted, I don't want to stick around any more.*

Besides the breakup itself, what devastated Fran was the discovery that her best friend was Ted's new girlfriend.

Miserable Alienation

Sometimes the note mainly shows how alone and misunderstood a depressed a youngster has been feeling. William, who had multiple learning disabilities and was essentially friendless, wrote:

> *I'm so alone. I can't stand being like this any more. Nobody understands me, and nobody ever will.*

Holly's mother and grandmother both suffered from depression, and in her senior year of high school Holly herself became terribly depressed—for no apparent reason. This is what's called endogenous depression, meaning a depressive illness that evolves from a person's biological or biochemical makeup, not from any particular shock or setback. Holly sank deeper and deeper into depression, feeling progressively more worthless and hopeless. Before cutting her wrists in a suicide attempt, she wrote:

> *I'm not sure when things started to change, but everything in my life rotted and fell apart. I was hoping things could be like they used to, but now I realize that will never happen. I have to put an end to this. I don't want to go on.*

"Forgiveness" as Blame

When a youngster's suicide note specifically forgives someone, that person usually "reads" the opposite meaning—namely, that the note is actually pointing a finger of blame.

Joseph, whose parents divorced when he was in kindergarten, never could accept the fact of the divorce.

All through his school years, he threw tantrums with both of his parents and their new spouses. The situation further deteriorated in his adolescence, when he started to drink and became involved in drugs. After a particularly violent dispute with his mother and stepfather, he succeeded in killing himself with an overdose of sleeping pills washed down with vodka. His note to his mother said:

> *I know you didn't mean what you said, and I know you can't understand how it made me feel. It wasn't your fault, and I'm not angry with you. I'm at peace now.*

Sexual Abuse

If there has been sexual abuse in the young person's background, her suicide note may allude to it in a roundabout way. Rena, whose father had molested her for years, wrote:

> *I used to think it was okay, but I didn't know anything back then. As I got smarter, it got more terrible. I thought I could live with it, but I was kidding myself. It's not possible. I have to go.*

As you can see, this note is cryptic. Rena deliberately wrote in a code she thought only her father would understand. When she wrote, "As I got smarter, it got more terrible," it was unclear whether she meant that the sexual abuse itself had escalated, or that her sense of revulsion had increased.

Rena tried to commit suicide by closing the kitchen doors and opening all the gas jets on the stove, but was saved by a neighbor who happened to stop by. In therapy, we learned that she had been putting up with her father's advances partly to keep him away from her younger sister.

Control

Occasionally a youngster's suicide note will be a desperate political statement. This happened a number of times during the Vietnam War era, when many bright, perceptive college students were passionately opposed to America's military intervention in Southeast Asia. One young antiwar protester who hanged himself in his dorm room left a note that said:

> *If the only way to make you see the truth is to meet violence with violence, then so be it.*

Another, who doused himself with gasoline and lit a match, left a suicide note addressed to the U.S. government. His note read:

> *My sacrifice is but a small gesture compared to the atrocities you are perpetrating upon the world. Please look at me and understand. It may be your only chance.*

Both of these young men mentally transformed their own country into a bad, disappointing parent who deserved to be punished. Both had "delusions of omnipotence": grandiose fantasies that their martyrdom would change the course of the war.

Attempts at control are the motivation behind suicide notes that say, in effect, "See what you made me do." Young people who are caught up in this type of thinking feel very weak and powerless. Committing or trying to commit suicide is their way of asserting personal power, of forcing others to take their ideas seriously.

Escape

A related phenomenon is the suicide note that mentions or hints at "rebirth" into a better world. Laurie, a highly intelligent but pessimistic and chronically unhappy child, became a strict vegetarian when she was 16. She spoke with deep conviction about animal rights and global responsibility, but was unable to persuade her parents and sisters to stop eating meat. Vegetarianism was the symbol of her struggle for control and autonomy. At age 17, following a series of fruitless arguments with her parents about meat-eating and other issues, Laurie took an overdose of pills in an unsuccessful suicide attempt. Her note said:

> *I don't really want to do this, but I know of no other way. I can't live in a world where I'm forced at every meal to witness human cruelty. It's time for me to find peace in another world.*

Unlike the antiwar protesters, Laurie was focused on herself and her own inner experiences. What she had in common with the protesters was her struggle to gain a sense of power and control by influencing other people's behavior. It's significant that she showed ambivalence about wanting to die ("I don't really want to"), and that the dose of pills she swallowed was too small to be lethal.

Revenge

As we said at the start of this chapter, some young people write suicide notes that are clearly messages of revenge. Richard, age 14, an angry delinquent who violently resisted anyone's attempts to rein in his impulsive behavior, had a shouting match with his stepmother when she refused to buy him a new 12-speed bicycle. Several hours later, he took her handgun out of the drawer of her bedside table and shot himself fatally in the mouth. His hastily scrawled note read:

> *I always hated you. Now you can suffer for a change.*

Adolescents in general are thought to have a deep conviction of their own immortality; this is what makes some teens more brave and daring than older, more experienced people. The kid who commits vindictive suicide seems to have an unusually limited understanding of death's finality. Richard's violent death did indeed cause his unfortunate stepmother to suffer, but of course he was not around to savor her anguish.

Cluster Suicides

On March 28, 1990, in the small town of Sheridan, Arkansas, 17-year-old Raymond Dale Wilkerson killed himself by gunshot in his own home, leaving no note. A month later, Thomas Smith, a 17-year-old junior at Sheridan High School, stood up in front of his history class, told a girl named Rhonda that he loved her, and fatally shot himself with a revolver he had hidden beneath his shirt. That night, Thomas M. Chidester, 19, a senior, shot himself to death in his grandmother's home, leaving a note that simply said: *I can't go on any longer.* The following morning, 17-year-old sophomore Jerry Paul McCool was found by his father, dead of a gunshot wound to the head. He left no note.

Investigators tried to find a common thread linking the four suicides, but without success. The Sheridan tragedies were an instance of cluster suicide, a phenomenon in which one individual's death leads other young people to commit copycat suicides. Cluster suicides, whether coincidental or part of a chain, have occurred in Alaska, Arkansas, California, Colorado, Illinois, Indiana, Massachusetts, Minnesota, Missouri, Montana, Nebraska, New Jersey, New York, Ohio, Oklahoma, Texas, Utah, Virginia, Wisconsin, and Wyoming. Some of the more recent examples:

- In April 1989, four teens took their own lives in Hot Springs, Arkansas.
- In 1987, in the New Jersey town of Bergenfield, four

teens committed suicide together by sitting in a running car inside a locked garage.

- In 1983 and 1984, a total of eight teens in Plano, Texas committed suicide.

What's the Explanation?

In trying to understand the suicidal youngster, it's necessary to take a hard look at the "copycat" factor.

Since adolescence is the time when kids form their identities and try to figure out who they are going to be as adults, teenagers are by nature very "groupy." By "groupiness" I mean an exquisite, image-conscious sensitivity to other teens and what they are doing and thinking. Groupiness is the reason colleges have fraternities and sororities; it's the reason we at Southwood Hospital emphasize group therapy sessions for teenagers.

Groupiness is also the reason why a kid who feels depressed and alienated is in truly desperate straits. Whereas an adult might tolerate or even like solitude, most teenagers thrive on a feeling of continuous connectedness to other kids. The lonely, misunderstood, or humiliated kid is severed from the reassuring peer contact that he so badly needs. More than other teens, he is likely to have suicidal thoughts and even plans for suicide.

Because adolescents are very sensitive to what they do in front of other kids, behavior is their first-choice way of communicating, of making statements to one another. Even for more verbal youngsters, behavior (rather than conversation) is the natural language of adolescence. Teenagers are dramatic; they act out their feelings much more than grownups do, and expect other kids to be the same way.

Suicide, of course, is a supremely dramatic act. And when a cluster of teen suicides occurs, it is best understood as a dramatic imitative phenomenon. In essence, a cluster suicide is a group suicide, even if the youngsters do not all die together. Young people in a cluster suicide carry adolescent imitativeness as far as it can go; they need to be like certain other kids, even if it means dying.

The Trigger Event

Does this mean that as soon as one young person commits suicide, all the other kids who knew him are apt to start thinking of suicide, too?

No, the situation is not nearly that direct. The four teenage boys who shot themselves to death in Sheridan, Arkansas were not close buddies. It would be a mistake to think that when one died, the next one committed suicide in a paroxysm of grief over the loss of a cherished friend.

Rather, each of these youths was essentially alone with his own personal story of emotional turmoil, distress, and desperation. When the first boy died, suicide suddenly became much more real to the second boy; it changed from an idea to a concrete fact. When the second boy died, suicide probably became a more viable option for the third boy—and so on in a tragic chain of events. The mounting suicides triggered imitative suicidal behavior in other *vulnerable* kids.

Personal Agonies, Public Acts

What about Thomas Smith, the second youngster in the cluster? This was the boy who told a girl "I love you" and then shot himself in front of his entire history class. If it's true that each teen in this particular cluster of suicides was tormented by his own private set of troubles, why would this particular youth choose to make his suicide so horrifyingly public?

As we have seen, young people have a deep need to appear acceptable to other kids. Even though the girl in question may not have been actively rejecting him, Thomas apparently *assumed* he could not possess her in a romantic way. It's my guess that, with his pride wounded by a sense of helplessness, he turned to suicide as a way to take action and reassert some control.

In effect, his suicide was a way of saying: "If I can't have this girl for my own then I don't want to live—and I want the whole world to know this." So deep was his desire to revalidate himself in the eyes of his peers that he was literally willing to die trying.

The Media: How Influential?

People often wonder if media reports of youth suicides encourage other teenagers to kill themselves. This was a controversial issue for many years. A few studies documented increased rates of suicide and auto deaths for several days following a highly publicized suicide, but there was never any way to prove a cause-and-effect relationship.

Based on the testimony of many adolescents who attempted suicide but did not die, most mental health professionals today believe that kids do not become suicidal because of a news story. It does appear, however, that media reports can reinforce suicidal tendencies in kids who are already preoccupied by such thoughts. Newspapers, TV broadcasters, and radio shows need not suppress coverage of teenage suicides for fear of "giving anyone ideas." Nevertheless, they should avoid glamorizing or sensationalizing the incidents, since this might appear to turn the suicide victims into romantic heroes. An impressionable, image-conscious youngster who was already vulnerable to suicide might see the victims as role models.

From a constructive standpoint, sensitive media treatment can be extremely helpful in *preventing* youth suicides. When one such suicide does occur, news briefs can alert troubled teens to hotlines and counseling centers that offer guidance and hope. In general programming, a show that portrays alternatives to suicide can have a positive influence on depressed, desperate young people. After watching a segment of *The Facts of Life* that dealt with suicide, one teenage girl wrote to the network to say that the show had made her decide not to kill herself.

6

Brains, Chemicals, and Fatal Decisions

Ray, age 17, survivor of a near-fatal auto crash:

> *As soon as I learned how to drive on the highways, I started having thoughts about how easy it would be to crash. There's this overpass a couple miles outside of town, and every time I went under it I would think to myself, all it would take is one lousy little turn of the wheel, and wham! Good-bye world. It was a spooky thought, but it was kind of like insurance, too—I felt like I would always have that as a way out if my life got bad.*

In fact, Ray's life did "get bad." Formerly an average student, he had been doing poorly in school that year, cutting a lot of his classes to hang out and party with other truant kids. The school was on his back, and so were his parents; his dad, who had a nasty temper, viciously knocked him around every time the vice-principal called or sent a note home.

For a while, Ray's major consolation was his girlfriend—a sweet, curly-haired 14-year-old named Shelley, who also liked to party and skip school. But in January, Shelley went away to a drug rehabilitation program, and six weeks later, when she came back, she told him she didn't want to be his girlfriend any more.

Ray tried to shrug it off, but the hurt went deep. Late one Friday night, drunk as a skunk after helping a few other guys down a case of beer, he took off in his parents' car, weaving through town and down onto the highway. Not having Shelley in the car beside him made him alternately depressed and furious. Suddenly he saw police lights flashing in the rearview mirror. In a rage, he stepped on the gas. As his speeding car approached the overpass, the usual thought popped into his head, and this time he swerved the steering wheel sharply to the left. . . .

Toying with Thoughts of Suicide

Viewed from the outside, the most mysterious and frightening aspect of a violent adolescent suicide is that crucial instant when the youngster actually goes ahead and does it—pulls the trigger, leaps off the rooftop, steers the car into a concrete wall. However, the act is almost never *purely* impulsive. Usually the kid has thought of suicide many times before.

As we saw in Chapter Four, many if not most people have an occasional suicidal thought. Especially for youngsters, who are still learning all about life, it's quite normal to wonder about death, about ways of dying, about how it would feel to die.

I remember having a brief suicidal thought of my own at the age of 13. I was a Boy Scout, and my uncle had just given me a handsome Swiss Army knife as a present. Sitting at the desk in my bedroom, I hefted the knife, opened one of the blades, saw how sharp and finely crafted it was, and suddenly wondered what it would feel like to cut myself with it. (In the back of my mind was something I had read about a Roman general who deliberately "fell on his sword" and killed himself.) I contemplated the delicate blue-green veins in my wrist, brought the Swiss Army blade near, and felt the thin cool pressure of steel on flesh. Then I pulled the blade away and closed the knife, knowing I didn't want to hurt myself and feeling a little foolish and guilty that I had even entertained the idea. I did not repeat or elaborate on the knife experiment. That was the end of it.

The Impulse Toward Suicide

In a depressed young person, however, the idle, once-in-a-while suicidal thought can start to occur more and more often. A particular object or landmark may trigger the thought, as the overpass did for Ray every time he drove down the highway. This is more than just a harmless daydream; it's a cause for worry.

Sometimes an unwanted suicidal thought become intrusive—popping up often at unexpected moments, interfering with the youngster's other thoughts. Gradually a preoccupation with suicide develops. A troubled, mistreated 15-year-old girl named Cherise told me that, for several months before coming to therapy, she kept having a mental image of herself plummeting from a high building. The thought got so distracting that she was unable to concentrate on anything for long. At least eight times, she went up to the roof of her apartment building and leaned over the edge, looking down and thinking how it would feel to fall from that height. "A couple of times," she said, "I almost let myself fall, just to put an end to that thought that kept running through my head."

What's the difference between someone like Cherise, who never did go over the edge of the roof, and a kid like Ray, who eventually steered his car into a concrete wall? What brings some youngsters to that fatal instant of decision, that final rush toward suicide?

Alcohol and Drugs: Good-Bye to Inhibition

Of the two teens mentioned, Cherise seemed much more obsessively suicidal than Ray. Yet something kept inhibiting Cherise from taking that final suicidal step. Time and again she peered over the edge of the roof, but each time, she refrained from jumping off. Operating within her brain was some kind of control: an awareness of danger, a measure of caution, a wish for self-preservation.

Ray, on the other hand, actually took the decisive step of crashing his car. In his mind, at least in that crucial instant when he swung the steering wheel, the controls were down. Ray's basic wish for self-preservation may have been just as strong as Cherise's—perhaps even stronger. But there was an important extra ingredient in Ray's story: alcohol. When he was speeding down the highway, Ray was quite drunk.

In our understanding of adolescent suicide we must face the fact that alcohol and drugs, which are widely available and quite popular, cause normal levels of control and inhibition to drop. In other words, even a very depressed or disturbed teen may be able to keep suicidal ideas in check—until normal controls loosen under the influence of alcohol, drugs, or a combination of both. Then, suddenly, it's much easier for the usually suppressed self-destructive impulse to make its way to the surface. In an instant of what may seem like liberating abandon, the kid makes the fatal move.

Danger for Users and Abusers

The stores are full of books about the dangers of teenage drug and alcohol abuse, and indeed this is one of the great social problems of our era. There's a direct connection between substance abuse and suicide: According to the *Encyclopedia of Suicide,* almost 50 percent of adolescents who commit suicide are drunk or high just before they die; that figure climbs to 75 percent for kids who make unsuccessful suicide attempts. Most people think of an alcohol and drug abuser as a kid who smokes pot on the way to school, gets drunk most nights of the week, steals from his mother's purse to buy crack on the streets, and so on. However, I want to point out that a kid who commits suicide under the influence is not necessarily a chronic abuser.

For the child who isn't used to drinking, one or two beers at a party may be quite enough to wipe out her usual inhibitions. If she has rarely or never smoked marijuana before, a couple of puffs on a joint may send her reeling. What happens next is unpredictable. If the high makes her feel warm and receptive, she may cozy up to the first boy who shows an interest in her. If it sends her into a tailspin, she may feel a panicky need to get away from people. However she behaves, it's guaranteed to be different from whatever is normal for her. She is feeling unleashed and impulsive. If she has been having thoughts of suicide, now may be the time she acts.

A Step Ahead of Depression?

Of course, adolescents who are chronic drug abusers are especially vulnerable to suicide. Teens often use alcohol and drugs to try to overcome feelings of depression, but sooner or later their effort backfires. Here's how it works:

Thrills and kicks are a temporary way to keep a step ahead of depression. As I mentioned in Chapter Five, kids are highly attuned to action of all kinds. The youngster who has feelings of hopelessness, despair, and self-loathing nevertheless knows that there is another "place" in life, a happy, satisfied place where existence is comfortable and rewarding. Since he's oriented toward action, he welcomes any activity that will carry him toward satisfaction and away from despair: "Tell me something hilarious! Let's do something fun! This will be a kick!" Drink and drugs attract him precisely be-

Some of the Drugs Kids Use

Alcohol, marijuana, and barbiturates ("downers) all depress the central nervous system. Under their influence, normal inhibitions diminish.

Tranquilizers or sedatives, such as Valium, also depress the central nervous system. Combined with alcohol, in excessive quantities, they can cause heartbeat and breathing to stop.

Cocaine and speed stimulate the central nervous system. They are extremely "disinhibiting," meaning they make rash, impulsive behavior more likely.

Crack is an inexpensive, concentrated, highly addictive form of cocaine. It creates an intense high often followed by paranoia.

PCP (phencyclidine, "angel dust") produces hallucinations and impulsive, violent behavior.

cause they feel good and loosen his controls. The chemical high itself, plus whatever reckless activity goes with it, promise him an intense, satisfying, depression-defying experience.

But thrills and kicks are dangerous in two ways. For one thing, they often involve all kinds of high-risk behavior. While drunk, stoned, or otherwise high, a kid may try anything:

- Walking in the dark across a high, narrow bridge
- Drag racing on empty streets
- Riding an open-sided elevator in an unfinished building
- Crusing at night through dangerous neighborhoods
- Playing "chicken" with cars or motorcycles
- Playing Russian roulette with a loaded gun

For another thing, the drugs themselves can be lethal.

Either an overdose of a single drug, or a combination of drugs that boost each other's effects, can kill.

The Sad Facts of Chemical Dependency

The farther a youngster slips into dependency on mind-altering chemicals, the greater the danger that he might take an overdose or a fatal combination of drugs. Close study of adolescent alcohol and drug abusers has shown that many of them progress quickly through four stages of abuse:

(1) Experimentation. Easy access to beer, marijuana, and other drugs, plus social pressure from friends, leads a teen to occasional "tryouts" of mood-altering substances.

(2) Recreational Use. The youngster becomes a "party animal," a regular social drinker or pot smoker, and feels somewhat cheated if he spends a whole weekend without getting a buzz at least once.

(3) Preoccupation. Getting high takes up increasing amounts of time, thought, and money—especially if the kid is using alcohol and drugs "medicinally" to mask such feelings as depression, anxiety, rage, or helplessness. He drops old interests and activities, and acquires new "druggy" friends. Schoolwork suffers.

(4) Dependency. At this point, the young person is physically addicted and needs drugs constantly just to ward off the sick, depressed feelings of a withdrawal syndrome. What started out as a quest for a "high" has deteriorated into a race against discomfort and even pain.

All the evidence indicates that vulnerability to alcoholism is an inherited trait; the same may be true for some kinds of drug dependency. Although no teenager can know in advance whether he has inherited the susceptibility, his risk is higher than normal if any of his blood relatives has an alcohol or drug dependency problem.

Smoking and Suicide: A Hidden Connection

Most teenagers would never dream there could be a connection between cigarette smoking and suicide. Yet surveys show that adolescents who smoke cigarettes are more likely than nonsmokers to move on to other drugs. As we have seen, much teenage suicidal behavior is drug-related. Thus, there is indeed an oblique connection between smoking and suicide.

A Biological "Push" Toward Suicide

As we've just seen, alcohol and drug use can stimulate the impulsiveness, or intensify and exaggerate the feelings, that can lead to suicidal acts. Laboratory research continues to demonstrate that biochemical changes within the brain accompany significant shifts in mood: In a very real sense, our brain chemistry *is* our mood, or at least its physical substrate. It's significant to note that, even in a youngster who does not touch beer or marijuana, an imbalance of various naturally occurring brain chemicals may generate self-destructive impulses. One of the inherent brain chemicals thought to play a role in suicidal impulses is serotonin.

In the 1970s, a Swedish doctor named Marie Asberg published a surprising finding: People who had abnormally low levels of serotonin in their cerebrospinal fluid (the natural fluid that bathes the brain and spinal cord) were peculiarly vulnerable to violent death by suicide (shooting, hanging, jumping). Other research scientists confirmed these results and added new findings:

- Some violent criminals also had low serotonin levels.

- Among people suffering from depression of various kinds, those who had low serotonin levels scored unusually high on psychological tests for anger.

An interesting fact emerged: depressed patients prone to violence tended to do very well on Prozac (fluoxetine), an antidepressant medication known to affect the brain's serotonin levels. Thus, serotonin, depression, and violence appeared to be linked in some way. So far, though, we are still unsure exactly how the connection works.

Serotonin is by no means the only focus of chemical research in psychiatry:

- Some people with depression are found to be low in norepinephrine, a different brain chemical.
- Some suicidal people who mutilate or cut themselves are low in beta-endorphins, still another type of brain chemical.
- The brain is now thought to produce as many as several dozen different chemicals that are likely to be involved in the variations and maintenance of mood. Many of these, or at least their balances in relationship to one another, may turn out to play significant roles in causing or inhibiting suicidal impulses.

Can A Kid Inherit a Tendency Toward Suicide?

There is impressive evidence that depression and suicidal tendencies can be inherited. Psychiatrists have long known that suicides can "run in families": a disturbed person with a close relative who committed suicide is himself at higher-than-normal risk for suicide. At first this seemed a mere matter of learning self-destructive behavior by example. But then came data showing that low serotonin levels—one of the biochemical "suicide markers"—run in families, too.

Manic-Depression and Suicide

In any discussion of teenage suicide, one particular psychiatric disturbance deserves special mention: manic-depressive disorder, which is also thought to be a brain-chemical disturbance. A kid with this disorder is subject to cyclical swings into two distinct types of mood: mania, which involves impatience, impulsiveness, expansiveness, and "hyper" behavior; and depression, which involves either sad, hopeless feelings or else belligerence and defiance. Psychiatrists used to assume that only adults could have these wide mood swings. However, research over the past decade has shown that some "juvenile delinquents" (also known as conduct-disordered youngsters), both boys and girls, are actually kids showing early signs of manic-depressive disorder.

Either mania or depression may increase a youngster's risk for suicide. In a full-blown manic episode, he might swipe his dad's keys and race the family car down the freeway at midnight, stepping on the gas even harder if the police try to pull him over. In a deep depression, he might jump off a bridge in a fit of self-loathing. In between mood swings, the kid may appear normal—or he may always seem to be tense, irritable, dissatisfied, and under stress.

Anthony Sherrod, the Georgia Tech basketball player who fatally shot himself in the head after failing to make the NBA, suffered from manic-depressive disorder. A close friend said, "He seemed like something was always bothering him." And Sherrod's coach commented, "He would worry about things, lie awake nights thinking about things you or I wouldn't give a second thought to." Sherrod sometimes drowned his problems in vodka. Once, after a night of drinking, he blasted repeatedly at the sky with his new .38-caliber revolver. Another time, after spending several days without eating or sleeping, he ran for more than eight miles and then collapsed. When the coach was called in, Sherrod lay on the floor and cried.

There's ample evidence that the tendency to develop manic-depressive disorder is inherited. I often hear parents say their troubled, violent kid is "just like his uncle" or "just like his grandfather"; without realizing it, they're pointing out the genetic nature of the illness. Physically, the trouble stems from abnormal ratios of those chemicals produced within the brain (neurotransmitters). Serotonin, dopamine, norepinephrine, and acetylcholine have been regarded as the most influential of these chemicals, but as research continues to uncover additional substances, the final number of significant compounds, as mentioned earlier, may be 20, 30, or more. Even a susceptible kid probably won't develop manic-depressive disorder, however, until he finds himself under unusual stress.

Fortunately, manic-depressive disorder is treatable. For some kids, especially those whose episodes of mania and depression are frequent and severe, the treatment of choice is ongoing daily doses of the medication lithium carbonate aided by additional medication when necessary. For others, including those whose mood swings are less frequent and/or not as severe, alternative treatment might be periodic courses of antidepressants and major tranquilizers such as Thorazine (chlorpromazine) or Stelazine (trifluoperazine), or an antiseizure medication such as Tegretol (carbamazepine) which has more recently been determined to promote mood stabilization in certain individuals. Diagnosing manic-depressive disorder is tricky, since the illness can take many forms and is easily confused with other conditions. That's why it's important for a kid with severe behavior problems to be evaluated by a psychiatrist (a medical doctor specializing in psychiatry), who will look beyond the disruptive behavior for causes that might be physical, or biochemical, as well as psychological.

Risk-Taking: Letting Someone Else Do the Job

Many adolescent suicides are reported as accidental deaths; when in doubt, a coroner will usually rule a young person's death accidental. A teenager's death is tragic enough in itself; when the cause is suicide, the family is torn apart by guilt as well as grief.

However, even a cursory look at teenage risk-taking reveals that the line between accident and suicide can be thin. The youngster who knowingly and repeatedly puts himself in life-threatening situations is acting out his ambivalence about death. He does not feel clearly that he wants to put an end to his life; on the other hand, the idea appeals to him on some level, at certain moments. Flirting with danger is a way of partly abdicating responsibility for himself. If the worst happens, he thinks to himself, then it won't really be his fault.

Let me share with you Brian's and Janet's stories, which are typical of a certain kind of teenage death that is neither pure suicide nor pure accident.

Brian's Story

When I was doing my medical internship, I saw an 18-year-old college student named Brian who was dead on arrival at the hospital emergency room; while high on the hallucinogenic drug LSD, he had leaped out of a sixth-floor dormitory window. Somewhat to my surprise, the county coroner ruled this an accidental death. He reasoned that this kid was under the influence of a powerful drug, probably had hallucinations, imagined that he was a bird or Superman, and didn't realize what he was doing when he jumped out the window.

But, I wondered, was the death entirely accidental? According to what his friends said in the emergency room, Brian had been feeling despondent for many weeks and had been taking a lot of LSD. My guess was that he was trying to stay high all the time, to keep a jump ahead of his despair. But on this one occasion, while his drugged mind was reeling, the balance of forces apparently shifted, pushing him to act on an impulse that proved fatal.

To use a different image, this young man had deliberately put himself in the path of death, and had finally been mowed down. Sure enough, his death looked accidental and was listed as such. But to my mind, this was not the same thing as a "pure" accident; by using LSD so heavily, Brian bore a great deal of the responsibility for putting his life in danger.

Janet's Story

I had already been in psychiatric practice for some time when I met the distraught parents of Janet, a 13-year-old girl who had recently died. Against her parents' advice, Janet had gone mountain-climbing with two friends in the dead of winter. Near the top of the mountain, she slipped down an icy slope and plunged over a cliff to her death. The death certainly looked accidental, even to the two friends who were eyewitnesses. Yet the parents were horrified when they found, on Janet's desk, an unfinished letter to a friend that contained these lines:

> *I hate my life so much ever since we moved here. Every day I wish I could find some way to die. I think about it all the time.*

For five months, ever since the family's move to a new state, Janet's behavior had been angry, defiant, and rude. Her parents were well aware of her behavior problems, but had not realized that these were her desperate attempts to override feelings of loneliness and depression. For Janet, the dangerous mountain hike had probably represented a way to act out her defiance and her terrible ambivalence about life and death. Once on the mountain, she lost her balance, both emotionally and in the literal sense—and the result was a terrible tragedy.

From Understanding to Prevention

In Part I, I approached the grave problem of adolescent suicide from an outsider's perspective, defining the issue and spotting some of the social forces that shape it. In Part II, I have moved closer to the suicidal kids themselves, showing how their deaths or near-deaths are misguided attempts to deal with life.

Defining the problem gives us a grasp of the issues; developing our understanding of the kids gives us empathy as well as perspective. Now it's time to consider what we, as adults, can do about this tragic, needless waste of precious young lives. That will be my focus in the third, and final, section of this book.

PART THREE

SPOTTING SUICIDAL KIDS AND HELPING THEM

7

Telltale Signs of a Suicidal Kid

From what you have read so far, you know that adolescent suicide usually doesn't just happen out of the blue. In most cases, the suicide or suicide attempt occurs after a buildup of despair. Often what's behind the despair is severe unhappiness and depression—caused by painful circumstances, disordered brain chemistry, or both.

However, depression in a teenager can be deceptive, because the only visible clue may be the behavior it generates. Usually teenage depression looks like something else: perhaps defiance and delinquency, or boredom and apathy. If a youngster you care about is depressed and perhaps suicidal, how can you tell? And how can you use your adult influence to help avert a tragedy?

Neither you nor anyone else, including a psychiatrist, can really be a mind-reader. Some adolescent suicides and suicide attempts are truly impossible to foresee and forestall. Don't make the mistake of thinking that every teen suicide is the result of inattention or indifference on the part of parents, friends, teachers, or counselors. That's simply untrue, and it's a destructive notion; it burdens the survivors with a needless load of guilt and bitterness.

That said, though, it's still true that in many cases a depressed young person who is considering suicide does give off warning signals—some of them faint, others clearer and more distinct. Since these signals are initially all you have to work with in attempting to ward off a possible suicide attempt, it makes sense to give each one a long, hard look. The three broad categories of signals are *verbal clues* (what the youngster says), *behavioral clues* (what the youngster does), and *life clues* (what's happening to the youngster).

What the Kid Says

"Maybe we should have taken him more seriously when he said he wished he could die." It's unfortunately common to hear this kind of remark from the friends of a young person who committed suicide. Teenagers sometimes *do* come right out and say they are thinking of suicide. On the other hand, they may express themselves ambiguously. If a child says (or screams) something like, "You just wait! You won't have me to kick around much longer!" he may be thinking of running away from home—or of committing suicide. Either way, since a teen runaway is also at increased risk for suicide, this kind of veiled threat deserves serious attention.

Because young people are struggling for independence and autonomy, a teenager is more likely to admit his suicidal thoughts to a trusted peer than to a parent. Often, the friend assumes this knowledge must be kept confidential. "Telling on" the suicidal buddy seems tantamount to betraying his trust.

Yet "telling" may be the very best way to get the troubled kid the kind of help he needs. Thus, you should encourage youngsters not to keep it to themselves when one of their peers starts talking of suicide. They should lose no time telling what they know to an adult in whom they have confidence: a parent or relative, for example, or a school guidance counselor, teacher, coach, minister, or doctor.

Of course, if you are the adult who receives these confidences, you must be prepared to act. Find out now what anti-suicide resources your community offers. Ask around to determine which school counselors or teachers are most adept at referring a troubled youngster to competent professional help. If the suicidal young person is not in school, find out how he can get help anyway. Then make sure he gets access to whatever help is available. Talk to his parents or guardians, if they are approachable. If not, talk to the youngster himself. Show him where he can go for guidance, and offer to take him there. Let him know your offer of help is genuine.

How the Kid Acts

As we have said, a teen who commits or attempts suicide has usually been depressed for some time, but the depression may have taken the form of aggressiveness or boredom rather than sadness. In an adolescent, any combination of the following signs may signal a depressed, pre-suicidal state of mind:

Physical Complaints

If a previously normal, well-adjusted kid suddenly starts to suffer from regularly occurring headaches, stomachaches, or arm or leg pains, this may be her physical expression of an emotional problem. It goes without saying that a doctor should first check thoroughly for any actual physical ailment: the youngster may genuinely have migraines, for example, or an ulcer, or an arthritic disorder. But if no physical illness is found, and the complaints continue, it may be time to consider the possibility of an emotional origin. This is especially true if the aches and pains are causing her to miss a lot of school and to spend an unusual amount of time by herself.

Difficulty Concentrating

One of depression's notorious effects is its erosion of the ability to concentrate. Depressed people have various ways of describing this. Some say it's like having cobwebs in their brain. Others say it's like seeing everything in dull colors and in only two dimensions. Still others say it's as if everything is of equal importance, so that they are unable to decide what is meaningful and what isn't.

Lack of concentration is a tremendous handicap in school, and almost always leads to a drop in academic achievement. But it's noticeable in the home, too. Some things to watch for:

- The young sports fan who suddenly turns off the TV set in the middle of a baseball game; he is no longer interested in seeing who will win.
- The avid young reader who suddenly abandons her novels after the first few chapters; she "just can't get into it" or no longer has the patience to keep reading.
- The kid who continuously complains that he can't concentrate on anything any more.

Neglect of Personal Appearance

If your young teenage son has always been slightly on the grubby side—if he still needs reminders to brush his teeth, clip his toenails, and swab the wax out of his ears—that's not a sign of depression. But if a kid suddenly shifts from casual to sloppy, or from sloppy to disgusting, that may indeed be a sign that, emotionally speaking, all is not well. As they mature, most teens grow increasingly conscious of their personal appearance; some make an absolute fetish of grooming themselves in a way they think will win their peers' admiration. Once a youngster develops this kind of appearance-consciousness, it's highly unusual for him to lose it. If he does lose it, depression, with its feelings of worthlessness and dulling of the normal powers of discrimination, is one possible explanation.

Sudden Alcohol or Drug Abuse

In Chapter Six I emphasized how harmful teenage alcohol and drug use can be. Even in kids who would not be classified as regular "substance abusers," getting high and losing normal inhibitions when they're in a vulnerable emotional state is sometimes all it takes to unleash impulsive, risky, potentially suicidal behavior.

Thus, it's cause for immediate concern if a normally sober and responsible young man suddenly starts to come home from parties roaring drunk, or if a generally level-headed and reasonable young woman suddenly starts imitating and running around with heavy drinkers and drug users. Such a youngster may be trying to self-medicate feelings of depression and despondency. As we have seen, this kind of amateur self-help is doomed to eventual failure—and may inadvertently contribute to a suicide attempt, whether intentional or seemingly accidental.

Trouble at School

Diminished powers of concentration are not the only way depression can affect a youngster's life at school. The depressed kid may react to his dark, hopeless feelings with rage, desperately and indiscriminately lashing out at the people and even the objects that surround him. It's as though depression is an evil force bearing down on him; he senses that if he can strike down this oppressive force, he will regain control and a feeling of freedom.

At school, a kid's efforts to strike back at depression can produce what we usually call "delinquent" behavior: theft, vandalism, class-cutting, truancy, defiance, threats—

and perhaps even physical attacks on teachers or on other students. The delinquent kid is correctly perceived as a menace to himself and others. What he needs is counseling and support. Understandably, however, most schools have a low tolerance for delinquency; the usual treatment for the chronic delinquent is punishment and, eventually, expulsion. Of course, getting kicked out of school merely intensifies the youngster's anger, humiliation, and feelings of depression and alienation.

Persistent, Endless Boredom

"I'm so bored!" What parent of a teenager hasn't heard this complaint, especially near the end of a lazy summer? But the boredom of a depressed youngster is not the simple result of temporary idleness. In fact, it's not regular boredom at all, but rather a continuous emotional bleakness, an internal atmosphere of hopelessness, an unending "What's the use?" feeling.

This so-called boredom is closely linked to the youngster's impaired ability to concentrate. A kid who is always "too bored" to go shopping, seek out friends, play the piano, or walk the dog is not really bored—more than likely she's depressed.

Withdrawal

A common sign of depression is withdrawal from friends, family, or a normal daily routine. I remember the following young people, former patients at Southwood Hospital, whose withdrawal had been severe enough to cause their parents to seek therapy for them:

- Sarah, age 15, who quit her wonderful drama club at the beginning of the spring semester and began coming right home after school every day to do nothing in particular. She developed a habit of rubbing her wrists with an eraser until the skin broke and bled.

- Cameron, age 13, who spent entire weekends lying on his bed listening to heavy metal music with gruesome lyrics. He smoked a lot of marijuana, and bought T-shirts and posters that featured images of skeletons.
- Kurt, age 19, a normally gregarious young man who lost his summer job as a camp counselor. The director of the camp had to ask him to leave midway through the season, because he kept walking off into the woods and leaving his group of youngsters unsupervised. When asked to pay closer attention to the kids, Kurt said he just couldn't. It turned out he was obsessed with thoughts of drowning himself.

Change in Eating or Sleeping Patterns

The brain's appetite control center (popular health articles sometimes call it the "appestat") is highly sensitive to emotions, and for good reason: it's located quite near the brain's emotion-processing center. People have long recognized poor appetite and weight loss as signs of depression. More recently, doctors have realized that some people react to depression by overeating. Thus, a teenager who undergoes a sudden dramatic weight change, either upward or downward, may be suffering from depression.

What complicates the issue is that body image itself affects the emotions. A depressed girl who puts on 20 pounds will probably get even more depressed as she discovers she can no longer fit into her clothes. In addition to dwelling on whatever original problems she had, she now starts to loathe herself for being a "pig" or a "glutton." If her dieting efforts don't produce immediate results, she takes this as further proof that her life is a hopeless mess.

Sleep, like appetite, can go either way. A severely depressed kid may sleep all day. On the other hand, he may have trouble falling asleep, remaining asleep, or he may wake up much too early in the morning and find he can't get back to sleep.

By itself, a disturbance of appetite or sleep is not necessarily a sign that a youngster is depressed. However, if both eating and sleeping disturbances develop simultaneously, and if the youngster is acting peculiar in other ways—withdrawing from friends, for example, or having temper tantrums—depression is a distinct possibility. For a kid caught in this situation, suicide may start to seem like a way out of despair.

Sudden Personality Change

Yet another giveaway of depression is an abrupt, inexplicable change in personality. If a girl who has always been outgoing suddenly loses all interest in seeing people and doing things, there's a good chance she may be depressed. Likewise, if an even-tempered guy suddenly turns so aggressive and irritable that parents and friends ask, "What's happening to you?" what's happening to him may be depression.

A sinister twist on this theme is that a seriously depressed kid who has always been somewhat sloppy may have an uncharacteristic fit of tidying up just before trying to commit suicide. You may recall from Chapter Four that Colleen, who slashed her wrists one morning, had spent the whole night straightening up her room. It was as if the decision to commit suicide had calmed her seething emotions and allowed her to focus on precise, concrete tasks.

In similar fashion, a youngster who has definitely decided on suicide may get all his affairs in order just before taking the final, fatal step—just as an older person might pay off all his debts, or hire a lawyer to draw up his last will and testament. A colleague once told me about a 14-year-old boy named Franco who gave away his beloved baseball mitt, and returned three cassettes he had borrowed from a friend, several hours before he hanged himself from a banister.

Likewise, in a severely depressed young person, a sudden spurt of energy and determination may signal a decision to commit suicide. Lynn, age 20, had been severely depressed, withdrawn, and inactive for many weeks, and didn't seem to be doing any better despite medication and counseling. One morning she bounced downstairs to breakfast humming and acting very energetic. This change was so dramatic that her mother, though pleased, felt somehow afraid to ask too many questions. It's highly likely that Lynn had just made up her mind to end her life; her eerie cheerfulness doubtless stemmed from relief and from a regained sense of purpose and control. Later that day she took a bus into the city, jumped off a bridge, and died.

What's Happening to the Kid

Doctors know that changes in brain chemistry sometimes cause unhappy, depressed feelings; they also know that stress and unhappiness sometimes produce biochemical brain changes. The chicken-or-egg question that puzzled psychiatrists throughout most of the twentieth century was this: Which comes first, the chemical changes or the depressed feelings?

At present, there's general agreement that the two phenomena are interrelated in such a way that either one can come first—an internal shift in brain chemistry can trigger feelings of depression, or an emotional blow can trigger the chemical changes associated with depression. Once such a dynamic interactive process is in motion the two components can reinforce each other, prolonging and deepening the depression.

So far, we don't have the technology to actually peer inside a youngster's brain and tell instantly if depression-causing biochemical changes are taking place. But we do

Kids at Highest Risk

Which adolescents are most likely to commit suicide? A kid is in the high-risk category if he:

- Is depressed
- Has a close relative who has suffered from depression
- Had a parent or sibling who committed suicide
- Previously tried to commit suicide himself

The more of these factors occurring together, the higher the risk of suicide; the kid in greatest danger of taking his own life has all four risk factors.

know that personal stress, especially when it involves a sense of loss, is particularly apt to make a kid depressed. Thus, if we know that a vulnerable kid is in a rough life situation, particularly one in which he has suffered a loss, we can interpret this as a red flag signaling a greater potential for a suicidal outcome. These are some of the personal stress factors that have been implicated in the development of suicidal crises in teenagers:

Parents Who Don't Care

If the parents don't care about the kid, the kid doesn't care about himself. One of my patients, a 14-year-old girl named Mary, had tried to commit suicide by overdosing on sleeping pills. As a young child Mary had been filthy, underfed, and dangerously neglected. Her mother was a young prostitute who had thought she "wanted a baby to play with," but who soon tired of all the responsibilities of child-rearing. Although a kind, responsible couple eventually adopted Mary and cared for her lovingly, the girl's self-esteem had been so badly damaged during those first crucial years of her life that she remained highly vulnerable to depression.

Parents Who Seem Like Tyrants

A kid whose parent forces him into a rigid, ill-fitting mold can either cave in or rebel; either way, he's ripe for depression. The poorly coordinated, bookish boy whose father insists on trying to make an athlete of him feels like an abject failure when he doesn't make the team. The spirited girl who carries on an active sex life, thumbing her nose at her parents' strict morals, may feel terrified, guilt-ridden, and desperate when she suddenly finds herself pregnant.

Loss of a Loved One

Often a teenager's strongest ally within the family is a relative. If his parents are impatient with him, or too preoccupied by money worries to give him much love and attention, perhaps a grandparent's wisdom and maturity serve as an emotional buffer. When the grandparent dies, the buffer is gone; understandably, the youngster finds this devastating.

Betrayal by a Friend

Since adolescents switch allegiances often, many teen friendships are highly unstable. The lonely kid who thought she had found an ally, but then discovered the "ally" was talking about her and ridiculing her behind her back, is deeply wounded. She may dwell morbidly on her presumed shortcomings, wondering if she is worthy of anyone's friendship.

Breakup with a Boyfriend/Girlfriend

To teens, ever apprehensive about whether they're normal, attractive, and acceptable, acquiring an official "friend-of-the-opposite-sex" can be the ultimate in gratification. Suddenly, after-school and Friday night dates liven up the week. She's shopping for new clothes, painting her toenails, changing her hairstyle; he's showering twice a day, tucking his shirt in, and wearing after-shave lotion even to school. Pleasing each other is what matters most in the world. When they break up, it feels like the end of the world. What's the point of looking good, acting clever, or showing enthusiasm any more? The abrupt change can signal a plunge into depression.

Loss of Status

A boy is thrilled to have a girlfriend because her allegiance confirms his identity as a desirable person. A girl gets a similar boost from having a boyfriend. When one jilts the other, the "jiltee" may feel the whole world is collapsing: "It's not just that I don't have a date any more—it's that everyone *knows* I don't have a date." The resulting shame and humiliation can be severely depressing.

Fitting the Clues Together

Life for teens is naturally full of ups and downs, so it's useless to worry about suicide every time a kid stamps her foot, stares into space, or skips a meal. As an adult, you need to develop a keen awareness of the adolescent's general state of mind.

If a youngster is talking about wanting to die, or if she is showing several of the signs of depression I've mentioned, or if she's under unusual stress from parents or peers—most especially, if *all three* of these warning categories apply—then it's time to get serious about the possibility of suicide, and to reach out to this troubled kid. How to reach out, and keep on reaching, is the subject of the next chapter.

8

Keeping Those Lines of Communication Open

When Is a Suicide Attempt for Real?

As you read and think about the many adolescents who make attempts on their own lives, you may long to reach out and comfort any kid who is so desperate. And yet, in all honesty, you may have a small, nagging doubt in your mind. Aren't some teenage suicide attempts just dramatic ways for kids to draw attention to themselves? How can anyone tell whether a bungled suicide attempt was "for real" or just a cruel manipulation—a gesture designed to make the kid's parents feel fearful and guilty?

Attempts versus Gestures

In trying to think clearly about this issue, it helps to know that psychiatrists do draw a distinction between the suicide attempt, which is "for real," and the suicidal gesture, which isn't.

According to the definition, a kid who survives a bona fide suicide attempt would have died if not for some fortuitous but unforeseen circumstance. I once met a

16-year-old boy named Jerome who rigged up a noose in his garage, slipped the rope around his neck, and jumped off a box—but didn't die. Because he had miscalculated by a mere half inch or so, his feet ended up touching the ground, preventing the pressure of the noose from breaking the vertebrae in his neck. Jerome's near miss deserved to be called a genuine suicide attempt. I also remember Anita, a 21-year-old grocery store clerk, who wrote a suicide note to her parents, took a couple of sleeping pills, went into the garage, closed the door, got into her car, turned on the engine, passed out—but did not die. What saved Anita's life was that the car engine stalled before she had breathed in enough carbon monoxide to kill her. Anita's brush with death, like Jerome's, met the definition of a true suicide attempt. It was a genuine attempt to die.

By contrast, a kid recovering from a suicidal gesture never intended to die. Usually, the suicidal gesture is a distress signal that uses the "language" of self-destructive behavior. Odalys, age 15, swallowed 12 aspirins in the girls' room at school. As soon as she began to feel sick and dizzy, she went to the school nurse and told what she had done. She said she didn't want to live—but the nonlethal dose of aspirin she took, plus her promptness in reporting to the nurse, suggested that this was a suicidal gesture rather than a real suicide attempt.

A nonlethal overdose of a modest amount of medication is quite a common suicidal gesture. Some gestures are more subtle. For example, Kara, aged 12, dug at her wrist with the sharp tines of a plastic fork until she drew a trickle of blood—not enough to endanger her life, but enough to greatly disturb those who saw her do it.

Kids' Feelings Afterward

I mentioned earlier that a suicidal kid is usually quite ambivalent about wanting to die. This becomes clear when you listen to what kids say they feel after making a suicide attempt, or even a suicidal gesture. Jerome, the boy who almost, but not quite, hanged himself in the garage, felt a tremendous sense of wonder and relief when he realized he was still alive; he said it was almost like being reborn. His dangerously close call convinced him that he really did not want to die. Kara had been feeling dazed, almost mesmerized, as she scraped open the skin of her wrist with the plastic fork; once she saw the blood begin to ooze, she suddenly "came to" and said to herself, "Oh my God, what am I doing?" As soon as she had slapped on a Band-aid, she said, she felt better, as if she had safely made it through a gruesome ordeal. Her mother and stepfather became extremely concerned and solicitous when they found out what she had done.

It's worth noting that the vast majority of teens who make suicidal gestures—roughly nine out of 10—are girls. Psychiatrists have different ideas about why this is so. My thinking is that our culture "permits" or encourages girls, much more than boys, to be dramatic in their efforts to influence other people's emotions. The reverse side of the coin is that many more boys than girls actually kill themselves: the ratio is about three to one. This may be the grim consequence of our culture's expectation that "real men" should be ruthlessly efficient and should never look back, while women may posture histrionically.

Parents' Anger

Darlene was 20 and unhappily married; shortly after giving birth to her second baby, she swallowed a bottle full of aspirin and wound up in an emergency room. When Darlene's mother got the call from the hospital, her face reddened. As soon as she had hung up, she began cursing and slamming dishes around the kitchen. When Darlene's father found out what the news was, he too went through a brief moment of cursing and shouting.

Strange as it may seem, anger is a fairly typical response in parents whose child has made a suicidal gesture. That's because the parents sense that the suicidal gesture was the kid's indirect way of communicating distress. They feel guilty, anxious, and ofttimes responsible for their child's distress—and they're angry at being made to feel that way! Aware of being manipulated emotionally, they feel like saying to their kid, "Dammit, stop this hysterical act! You're just doing it to upset me and make me feel guilty!"

Constructive Response

Parents can't help feeling angry, of course, but they can move beyond anger. Their first thought may be, "Let's not pay any attention to this stupid act she's putting on, or it will just encourage her to repeat it." True enough, if they ignore the suicidal gesture they will temporarily avoid being manipulated by their child. However, since they also fail to respond to the message she was trying to convey, there will be no resolution of the problem.

A more helpful way for parents to respond to a suicidal gesture is to treat the gesture as a very serious communication, and try to get a dialogue going with their youngster. Using whatever words come naturally to them, they should convey to their child this message: "Okay, you've succeeded in getting my attention. I realize that you are upset about something, and I feel for you. Now, let's talk. What is it that's bothering you? What do you need emotionally that you aren't getting?"

A kid makes a suicidal gesture because she feels she can't communicate in any other way. In essence she is saying, "If I can't tell you how much I'm hurting, then

I've got to show it to you this way." She's giving her parents, or whichever people care most about her, an opportunity to open up new lines of communication—and keep them open. Now I'd like to address the question of how a grownup can reach out and establish communication with a young person who is, or might be, suicidal.

Talking to a Suicidal Kid

How likely is it that you will someday encounter a suicidal kid? More likely than you might think. Studies show that at any given time, 10 to 15 percent of all adolescents are suffering from some degree of depression—and as we have seen, depression forms the background for most suicidal thoughts, gestures, and attempts. Thus, when you sense that a teenager is sad, maladjusted, disruptive, or otherwise disturbed, there is at least some chance that the kid has been having thoughts of suicide.

But how can you know whether a youngster is actively suicidal? The answer is, in many cases you can't. What you *can* do, though, is reach out to a troubled youngster and offer to *listen* to his problems. If he does indeed tell you that he has been having self-destructive thoughts, you'll know that your suspicions were justified.

What happens next depends on you and your relationship to the youngster. If he is your own child, you can offer to help him by listening, understanding, and even advising, but enlist professional help if the going gets rough. If he isn't your child, you are of course not responsible for trying to help him solve his problems. However, since you're probably interested in being a good citizen and doing what's right, you can make sure he knows where to turn with his troubles. That's a way to discharge your responsibility honestly and helpfully.

Opening Lines

Your son Tad, age 14, has you worried. His grades are slipping, he's morose and irritable, and for more than a month he has stayed away from the two or three boys who are normally his good friends. Among the kids at Tad's middle school, there's a nasty little underground routine called "taking the wimp test." To pass the "test" you rub the skin on the back of your hand with an eraser and keep on rubbing until the skin wears away and bleeds. Usually a kid does it only once, to prove he isn't a wimp. But you notice that Tad keeps on taking the wimp test. His forearms, his wrists, and the backs of both his hands are covered with ugly scabs which are wimp-test abrasions in various stages of healing. You're afraid Tad is quite depressed, and this self-mutilation makes you wonder if he might even be suicidal.

"I've been concerned about you lately, Tad. I know you must be hurting. You seem like you're in a lot of pain." Often a simple, empathic opener of this sort is all it takes to start the conversation. You don't need to say anything fancy or high-flown; you don't need to rehearse your lines to make sure they come out right. The idea is just to let Tad realize that you are genuinely aware of his pain.

Showing You Care

The next step is to convey your caring. Of course you love your son, but perhaps it's rare for you to come right out and tell him that in so many words. Since Tad is depressed, he is locked away inside a kind of shell. Your aim is to tap gently on that shell until you make a little hole in it.

"I care about you, Tad, and I worry when I see you so closed up inside yourself." Your aim is not to make demands on Tad's emotions, but to reassure him—to let him know that even if he feels all alone with his problems, he doesn't have to remain alone.

Projecting Empathy

It's not just that you care in some abstract sense; Tad's depression actually affects you emotionally. It's as if his pain feels like your pain. Since this is true, why not let him know it?

"I sense how bad you feel inside yourself, and I can feel your distress." The kid who is depressed may suffer acutely from the feeling that no one can possibly understand how bad he feels. By projecting empathy—the capacity to put yourself in someone else's emotional shoes—you break through that terrible isolation.

Lending an Ear to Listen

You know that Tad is under some kind of serious strain, but you're unsure what the underlying problem is. If you're going to help him, you'll have to know what's on his mind. This is the time for you to invite him to share his thoughts with you.

"Can you tell me what's been bothering you lately. Are you able to talk about it at all?" Don't expect that Tad will give you a full, coherent analysis of his depression. He's probably very confused in his own mind about what he feels and what has been happening to him. Just *listen* carefully to what he says, and accept it without protesting. Remember that in all likelihood he'll find it helpful just to open up to you.

Offering Hope

The primary ingredient of any and all psychotherapy is hope. Once you see where the problems are, the best thing you can do for Tad is to offer him hope that things can get better, that his problems are almost certainly not insurmountable, and that he has you as an ally.

You may have an impulse to try to argue Tad out of his depression by giving him reasons why he shouldn't be depressed. Resist that impulse! Depression was not a state of mind he chose rationally; rather, it crept up and overtook him. If he feels you can't accept his bad feelings at face value, he'll stop sharing, and the dialogue that you have just begun will collapse.

Instead, let Tad know that you find his feelings understandable. Often that's all he will need in order to start feeling better. If there is some concrete help you can offer, now is the time to do it.

Wrong Way:

- "But Tad, you shouldn't fall apart just because you didn't make the team."
- "What do you really care if that dumb Sherrie wouldn't go to the dance with you?"
- So what if you have a little acne?"
- "If your friends really put you down because of the clothes you wear, I think you ought to look for a new set of friends."

Right Way:

- "That must have really shaken you when Alan made the team and you didn't."
- "I know how awful it feels when someone you really like rejects you. Did I ever tell you about the first time it happened to me?"

- "Acne can be embarrassing, I agree. I'll bet Dr. Grannon can give you some medicine that's stronger than what you've been buying."
- "I never bought you trendy clothes—I never knew how much they meant to you, and I felt they were too expensive. But maybe you and I can start watching for special sales."

But What If It's Not Your Kid?

So far, so good. But what if the depressed youngster you're concerned about is not your own child? There are many possible scenarios, and appropriate ways to handle them.

The Child of a Friend or Relative

Perhaps you have long enjoyed a good relationship with this youngster. In that case, it's totally appropriate for you to extend yourself to the kid, much as if you were the parent. "Patti, what's up? Lately it seems like you're upset all the time. Remember how you always used to have a joke for me? You just don't seem like yourself these days. Can you tell me what's bothering you?" Of course, you still have a responsibility to alert Patti's parents that you think something is wrong. If you have elected to talk to Patti, you may want to tell them that, too.

Perhaps you wouldn't dream of talking to Patti without first asking her parents' permission; much depends on your own values, how well you know her parents, and how you sense they would react. If you do register your concern, and Patti's parents are responsive, they may be perfectly able and willing to start the necessary dialogue with her. The important point is that *anyone* who can reach out to Patti should do so.

The Parents Realize the Problem, But Don't Know What to Do

Frequently the parents will be well aware that their child is going through rough times, but feel helpless to intervene. In that case, you might suggest that they get the support of a professional. Do some research on your own; find out what the possibilities are in your area—counselors, a clinic, a family service agency, suicide "hot lines"—so you can give the kid's parents something tangible to work with: a name, a phone number, perhaps a recommendation from a friend.

Meanwhile, the kid's peers may be a source of hope and help. Many schools nowadays have formal peer intervention and counseling programs, which in many cases grew out of concern over the problem of teenage suicide. For a troubled kid, it may be much less threatening to talk with another youngster than to open up to an adult. Peer counselors are not mental health professionals, of course, but they can refer a kid with problems to an appropriate adult who is willing to help.

A Kid Whose Parents Don't Like You

Maybe you don't know the kid very well, but from superficial encounters with him you can tell that he is very troubled. In this case, if you don't feel comfortable reaching out to engage him personally, you should definitely let his parents know that you are quite concerned.

Perhaps Rocky's belligerence and heavy drinking worry you, but you are at odds with his mother. If possible, express your concerns to his father. However, if his father is not around, you might have to deal with his mother after all. "Look, I know you don't like me, but my call has nothing to do with that. I know you care about Rocky, and you can take this for what it's worth, but I am very concerned about him." She may immediately try to distance herself from you, so in order to be effective, make your comments as descriptive and credible as possible: "He used to be so easygoing and approachable. My own kids are worried about how he's acting these days."

If the mother still minimizes, negates, or denies all of her son's obvious signs of depression, your next step could be to notify the school. Your own children may be able to help you make contact with the right teacher or counselor. "I have noticed this about Rocky, but I myself find Rocky's mother inaccessible. Maybe you could get involved." If school is not a possibility, then try approaching some other person who has been influential in Rocky's life—a coach, perhaps, or a member of the clergy, or a doctor.

No Adult Seems to Care About the Youngster

Unfortunately, there's a possibility that the depressed, potentially suicidal youngster really is emotionally abandoned and alone in the world. If that's the situation, you can still do something to help. Virtually every community in the United States has representatives of social service agencies (in California the organization is called Child Protective Services; other states have other names for the same thing). If you are very concerned about the kid's emotional state; if her parents seem inconsistent, unavailable, unaware of her problems, or unwilling to help; if the youngster seems to have no relatives, no good friends, and no teacher, coach, or doctor to provide support, then you could get in touch with the social service agency. "I see a kid who appears very troubled, and I can't reach her family at all. Can something be done for her?"

Another possibility, if you feel up to it, is to reach out to the youngster yourself and try to establish communication. This way, you temporarily become a significant social support. Tell her there are places where she can get help. Ask if you may make an appointment for her, and perhaps take her there. You aren't proposing to solve her problems for her, but you are acting as a bridge or a link in a supportive network, leading her to professionals who can intervene and help her to make life more bearable.

Should You Mention the Word "Suicide?"

Rest assured that you will *not* cause a youngster to commit suicide by bringing up the word "suicide" in conversation. It just doesn't happen that way. Suppose that you are talking with a kid and he acknowledges that he has been "feeling lousy, feeling shitty." It's okay for you to ask, "How bad is it really, Jim? Is it so bad that you've thought about hurting yourself? Have you even thought you might not want to be around any more?" If Jim's answer is "yes," that will merely confirm your suspicion that it's urgent to get professional help for this troubled kid. Also, the very fact that you asked the question is likely to have a relieving and reassuring effect on Jim as he starts to feel more understood and less isolated.

Of course, you may be uncomfortable raising the issue of suicide with a kid. But that's okay, too. You can keep the conversation much more general: "I know you're feeling very troubled, Jim, and I want you to know that there are people who can help you with the kinds of things you're feeling (or problems you're telling me about)." If you stop at that point, and refer Jim to a professional, you will still have played the part of the "good neighbor" and made an important contribution.

Be Genuine

Probably the most important thing in talking to a possibly suicidal kid, or reaching out to anyone in serious emotional distress, is this: Be genuine. As you talk with a troubled youngster, let your words be real and honest, and let her words guide the conversation. As she talks, try to identify with what she is saying, literally putting yourself in her shoes. The more accurately you can read her emotions, the more likely it is that you will truly understand her pain. Encourage her to communicate, share, convey what is going on in her mind, and then try as hard as you can to hear and understand what she is telling you. Never let yourself be phony or artificial. Don't say, promise, or predict things you can't really know or control. Don't exaggerate, and don't say things just for effect. Be real.

If you jump the gun by asking, point-blank, "Are you thinking of suicide?" you may put her off. But if she feels your genuineness and empathy, and gradually develops enough trust to admit to you, "I've never felt so desperate," then the issue of suicide essentially comes up by itself. At that point, having won her confidence, you are poised to direct her gently to someone who can help her out of her distress.

9

How Professional Treatment Can Help

Now I'd like to talk about the needs of the youngster who has just attempted suicide—who has narrowly escaped death by hanging, shooting, drowning, overdosing, or any other method. What's the appropriate treatment? Who should give it? When? How?

Emergency Room Decisions

Eliza, 16 and miserably depressed, went to pieces after breaking up with the boy she had been seeing. While no one was home, she went into the bathroom and swallowed a large number of her mother's antidepressant tablets, practically a whole month's worth, in an attempt to die. Her parents, returning home from work around 9 p.m., found her lying comatose on her bed. A suicide note lay on the nightstand.

Paramedics brought Eliza to the emergency room of a large city hospital, where she underwent gastric lavage ("stomach-pumping"). She spent the next days in intensive care receiving respiratory assistance, heart monitoring, and medication to raise her blood pressure. The attending physician, nurses, and psychologist at the hospital talked with Eliza as she recovered. Because they agreed that she was still potentially suicidal, they recommended special hospital-based psychiatric treatment, and sent her to Southwood Hospital.

Not every teenager who attempts suicide needs treatment in a psychiatric hospital. Some kids who survive a suicide attempt, like Jerome whom I mentioned in Chapter Eight, are so profoundly affected by the experience, so relieved to be still alive, that they feel "reborn." Youngsters like this are usually sent home after arrangements are made for follow-up outpatient therapy. But Eliza's close call definitely did not make her feel relieved, grateful, or reborn. At the Southwood intake office, we found that she was filled with self-hatred, furious at her parents, and enraged that she had "screwed up" the attempt on her life.

What About Payment?

Eliza arrived at Southwood in an ambulance, followed by her parents. While a professional counselor was giving Eliza an intensive half-hour assessment, a social worker interviewed the parents about their daughter's background. Eliza's parents were relieved to learn that their health insurance would pay for psychiatric hospitalization (as most health plans do).

Since Eliza did seem to need hospital treatment, a staff member phoned me to explain the circumstances. I confirmed the evaluation, and gave instructions to admit Eliza at once to our adolescent psychiatric unit. I made an appointment to meet and talk with her a few hours later, after she'd had a chance to size up her new surroundings.

You may be wondering: What would Southwood Hospital have done if the family hadn't been covered by health insurance? As a private proprietary hospital, Southwood derives its income solely from the payments of patients and their health insurance plans. Yet we at

Southwood would never turn our backs on someone like Eliza. When a patient has no insurance, as sometimes happens, we care for her temporarily, and keep working with her parents until we find an appropriate facility that has the funding to care for uninsured patients.

Parents as Treatment Allies

At Southwood, the parents of a young patient are essential allies in her treatment. When Eliza was admitted, her parents had an interview with a social worker. They told about themselves (Polish immigrants who worked long hours at various jobs), their children (Eliza's development, as well as that of her mentally retarded older brother and her younger sister), and the way Eliza had been acting lately (she had always been a poor student; this year she had started running with a wild crowd, skipping school and antagonizing teachers).

They had been trying to crack down on her, they said, but she only got worse. Her father acknowledged that he occasionally had to slap her. Her mother said she had been withholding Eliza's allowance as a punishment. There were frequent violent arguments. Both parents were distracted by problems with their mentally handicapped son, and by money worries. Eliza's suicide attempt had stunned and terrified them; although they didn't like to admit it, they also felt angry and humiliated.

Before they left Eliza at the hospital, the parents learned something about the program their daughter would be entering, and found out that family therapy was part of the program. They made an appointment to come back in a few days for a family session.

Getting Started

Like most young patients entering the adolescent unit, Eliza was furious at being put in the hospital. But once her parents left and she realized she was stuck, she began to cooperate, glumly and reluctantly, with the various nurses and other professionals and staffers she encountered.

The whirlwind of activity in the first few days yielded interesting results.

As the *psychiatrist* who admitted her, I determined that Eliza was severely depressed. I prescribed an antidepressant medication that I hoped would help her emerge from her acute emotional distress. I also learned that sexuality was a major focus of arguments between Eliza and her parents. Eliza seemed to have a fair amount of insight into her own problems, which was a hopeful sign.

A *pediatrician,* specializing in adolescent medicine, examined Eliza and found out that she had already had an abortion. She talked with Eliza about boys and sexuality, and assessed Eliza's knowledge about reproduction and contraception. (Subsequently, at a treatment team meeting, the family therapist and I talked about the pediatrician's findings and decided how we could best approach the important subject of sexuality with Eliza's parents.)

Incidentally, the pediatrician also found that Eliza was quite nearsighted, and arranged for her to get glasses.

A *psychologist* who administered a battery of psychological tests discovered that Eliza swaggered and boasted to cover up deep feelings of inferiority and shame. She had such a negative concept of herself that she despaired of ever meeting either her parents's or society's expectations. Basically she was depressed because she was convinced she would never be a worthwhile, valuable person.

The tests showed that Eliza's intelligence was in the average-to-above-average range. Her verbal skills were quite good; her math skills somewhat less so; her motor skills (eye-hand coordination abilities) were distinctly poor. However, as I had noticed when I first met her, Eliza was good at abstract thinking, and already had some insight into her problems. This suggested strongly that she could benefit from psychotherapy and various other components of the treatment program.

Somewhat later, in an interview with Eliza's parents, a *social worker* took an exhaustive psychosocial and developmental history that helped explain the familial and social context of Eliza's depression. The social worker also steered Eliza's parents toward a special vocational school for the retarded older brother.

An *occupational therapist* did a visual-motor assessment and found that Eliza's physical sense of balance was faulty. This shed light on the test results demonstrating her poor eye-hand coordination. It helped explain Eliza's dread of athletics, her long history of failing grades in physical education, and some of the difficulties she had encountered at school and with her peers. The occupational therapist prescribed exercises to help Eliza improve her coordination.

A *speech and language therapist* found that Eliza's expressive and receptive language skills and abilities were well above average for her age and level of development.

The special *teacher* from Southwood Academy—a private, fully accredited school that operates within the walls of the hospital—created an individualized educational plan to accommodate Eliza's unequal verbal and math skills. Eliza began to take pride and satisfaction in her schoolwork.

A *recreational therapist* who did a vocation, interest, and hobby inventory noted that Eliza had impressive artistic talent. He introduced her to modeling clay, a medium that genuinely captured her interest. Eliza immediately began turning out touchingly delicate statuettes, many of them variations on a mother and baby theme. The recreational therapist also recommended that she participate in games that didn't outstrip her coordination limits.

Nurses, who play a major role at Southwood, were the first professionals to actually engage Eliza in the treatment program. They started by doing a nursing assessment: a total inventory and outline of significant facts about her. Then they gave her an orientation, introducing her to the various activities in her schedule. Nursing staff, and in particular her primary counselor, stayed in close personal contact with her throughout her treatment program. They acted as role models, showing her by example what the standards were for living successfully in the treatment community and hence, by extension, outside the hospital as well. They provided feedback and encouragement, and counseled her on topics as varied as relationships, sexuality, and nutrition. The nurses also did occasional blood and urine tests until I was satisfied that Eliza was receiving the right type and dosage of antidepressant medication, and that she was physically and medically fit.

Getting to Know the Other Kids

As the flurry of evaluations and examinations subsided, Eliza began to slip into the daily routine at Southwood: up at 7:30 a.m. for washup, bed-making, and room tidying, breakfast at 8, community meeting at 8:30, school at 9, group therapy at 11, lunch at noon. Then exercise at 1, individual counseling at 1:30, school again at 2, occupational therapy at 4, general meeting at 5, dinner at 6, family sessions or other group activity at 7, games and indoor recreational therapy at 8, journal writing at 9, and lights out between 10 and 11 depending on the level of responsibility earned.

At first Eliza was too upset and resentful to pay much attention to anyone else. But as the closely scheduled routine began to shape her life, she felt increasingly open to and involved with the 25 other kids in the program.

Not every kid on the adolescent psychiatric unit is there because of a suicide attempt. This unit accepts youngsters with a variety of emotional and psychiatric problems; the common factor is that all the patients are adolescents. Because teenagers are so "groupy," so tuned in to others their own age, they thrive on therapy that involves them with their peers. Eliza, who is white, first got to know LaKenya, 15, a crack-addicted black girl from a ghetto neighborhood, who arrived on the unit the same day she did. For a few days the two of them formed a "newcomers" subgroup. However, because LaKenya spent most of her time in the program's special track designed for drug-abusing kids, Eliza usually saw her only at meals and community meetings.

A little later, Eliza found herself curious about Eddie, a muscular, belligerent 17-year-old Hispanic kid whose arms bore scars from knife fights. She paid little attention to Hong, an expressionless 13-year-old Oriental boy who never said anything and didn't seem to have any friends. On the other hand, she secretly admired 16-year-old Lydia, beautiful and theatrical, who occasionally shouted and wept for no discernible reason. She was interested in curly-haired Tony, 15, a diabetic youngster who loathed his special diet and sneaked candy whenever he could. She initially felt contempt for Magda, 14, who was so anxious in group sessions that she trembled and lost her voice. And she was sorry for LeRoi, 17, who had lost both parents and a brother in an apartment house fire, and who was so freaked out and distracted that he didn't make much sense when he talked.

What Good Did the Program Do?

As the days turned into weeks, Eliza perked up visibly. The antidepressant helped lift her out of the depths of her depression. The close contact with the other kids, and the frequent group discussions about emotions and relationships, opened up a whole new vista for her: never before had she had such a vocabulary to talk about what she, and others, were feeling inside.

The program included some sessions on alcohol and drug use, and why kids should avoid it. Eliza was a little skeptical at first, but the testimony of kids who were trying to kick addictions eventually made an impression on her. She ate and slept well, color returned to her cheeks, and she took a renewed interest in clothes and makeup for herself. She came to like some of the kids on the unit. Others she disliked, but when they bothered her she learned to let them know how she felt without starting a fight.

She did well with her schoolwork, thanks to the specially tailored lessons (and the stylish new glasses!). In art therapy, she took great satisfaction in making her expressive clay sculptures. To her total surprise, she also enjoyed the gardening sessions that were offered, and she actually had fun in sports events led by the recreational therapist. In assertiveness training groups, she practiced expressing herself to the other kids by saying clearly and directly what was on her mind.

Meanwhile, she and her parents were developing new ways of relating to one another. In family sessions, she learned to talk more frankly with them about issues that bothered her: their seeming lack of interest in her; the disproportionate amount of time they spent on her handicapped brother; the way they spoiled her manipulative younger sister; the inescapable fact that her father drank too much and periodically abused her mother. The social worker was able to persuade Eliza's father to start going to meetings of Alcoholics Anonymous, and to interest Eliza's mother in Al-Anon meetings. Eliza began learning that some of her expectations of her parents were unrealistic. She also started to understand how she contributed to the communication problems within the family.

By the end of her five week stay at Southwood, Eliza had emerged from her depression fairly well. She was no longer having thoughts of suicide. Often, in fact, she was actually cheerful; she seemed to have a new, expanded perspective on life. Just before she went home, she signed a contract with her parents, promising to attend school regularly and do her homework without prompting. Her parents assured the counselor that they would talk, rather than strike out physically, if Eliza did something that displeased them.

After the Hospital

For some time after leaving Southwood, Eliza continued to see a counselor once a week, and to join her parents, brother, and sister in a weekly family therapy session. After a few months, I tapered her off her antidepressant medication without incident. The transition from the hospital back to her home was not entirely smooth, but now that she had someone to talk to she was able to handle her problems constructively.

For example, she found she still had trouble saying no when friends offered her beer and drugs. Eventually, however, following the counselor's advice, she joined a young people's AA group where she found encouragement to stay straight. Back at school, she used her newfound skills productively. Her report cards began to look better, and her self-confidence continued to improve. She cut down to one counseling session every two weeks.

Her schoolwork continued to be satisfactory, and she discovered a new set of friends. With her father beginning to take a serious interest in AA for himself, her home life grew more tranquil. A year after her suicide attempt, Eliza decided she no longer needed regular counseling sessions. She agreed to keep in touch if she wanted or needed to. She has been doing well ever since. Suicide is no longer on her mind at all.

Does It Always Turn Out So Well?

Although Eliza's story is fairly typical, not every suicidal teenager who spends time at Southwood Hospital emerges from the program transformed and lives happily every after. If a kid is still depressed, withdrawn, or overly impulsive, even after a number of weeks in the hospital, she may be transferred to a residential treatment facility. This is a live-in program, not unlike the hospital's adolescent unit, with 24-hour supervision. Unlike the hospital, however, it has unlocked doors and significantly less staff, and the youngsters are there on an entirely voluntary basis.

Even if his hospital stay has gone well, a youngster with absent or uncaring parents may move on to residential treatment, a group home, or a foster-family placement rather than return to an unsupportive or noxious home environment. Hong, the withdrawn boy Eliza met on the adolescent unit, was an orphan; he had been living with his drug-addicted older brother before coming to the hospital. After his discharge from Southwood, he spent 12 months in residential treatment; he is now living in a foster home, where he seems to be thriving. He is slowly overcoming his dread of talking to people, and has made several friends at his new school.

Help When It's Needed

Suicide, as I have described it throughout this book, is a solution born of desperation: an idea that occurs to a kid when life seems so ugly and pointless that it makes no sense to go on. There are several possible avenues of help for an adolescent who seems depressed, despairing, and possibly suicidal. For one kid, a kind word from a caring friend or grownup will be enough to put life's problems back in perspective. For another, regular sessions with a skilled professional will be necessary. For the very disturbed and dysfunctional teen, especially one who is profoundly depressed or who abuses alcohol and drugs heavily, it may take intensive treatment in the adolescent program of a psychiatric hospital to push back the tragic spectre of self-inflicted death.

As a hospital-based psychiatrist, I'm accustomed to seeing and talking with those suicidal teens who are the most desperate: the ones who actually swallowed the overdose, jumped off the bridge, cut open the veins in their wrists. We at Southwood, and professionals at other psychiatric hospitals throughout the country, stand ready to help these troubled kids find their way back to stability, self-confidence, and hope. I sincerely wish you never encounter a suicidal kid who needs the kind of facilities we offer. But if you do, I hope this book has shown you how to direct such a kid to help before it's too late.

Adolescent lives are precious. We can't afford to let a single one self-destruct. As well-informed adults, we can all share in a partnership of hope: looking out for our young people, spotting the signs of self-destructive or suicidal behavior as they occur, and most importantly, stepping in to offer a sympathetic ear and a helping hand.

Common Myths About Teen Suicide

Myths About Suicide and Society

Myth: Suicide is most common among rich, jaded white kids. Or: Suicide is most common among poor, deprived black kids.
Reality: Adolescent suicide cuts across all race and class boundaries. The red flag for potential suicide is not color or social status, but *depression;* the suicidal adolescent is likely to suffer from ongoing feelings of hopelessness, boredom, loneliness, worthlessness, and despair.

Myth: Women's liberation is the reason why there's more teenage suicide now than in the past. If mothers stayed home instead of going out to work, kids would be happier.
Reality: The teen suicide rate in the United States began to rise in the 1960s, well before mothers of young children flocked to the workforce. Clearly, other social forces were pushing teenagers toward suicide at that time; among these were family mobility, divorce and family disintegration, the Cold War, and the emerging threat of nuclear holocaust, to name a few. A kid who spends many hours at home unsupervised may indeed get lonely and depressed—but 24-hour surveillance by

his mother is only one of many possible forms of supervision.

Myth: If more families believe in God and paid attention to their religion, fewer kids would commit suicide.
Reality: The family that takes its religion seriously may well be closer and more cohesive than the family that doesn't. However, parents who are rigid and inflexible in their religious beliefs may wind up alienating their teenager when she reaches the point of needing to establish an independent identity. People do have spiritual needs, and religious affiliation and training can be deeply meaningful. However, parents should know that adolescents usually question religious doctrine sooner or later, and that this is a normal, healthy state in their development.

Myths About Alcohol, Drugs, and Suicide

Myth: Drugs may have helped cause the epidemic of teenage suicide, but not alcohol. Kids got drunk in the old days, and nothing ever happened.
Reality: It's a big mistake to consider teenage drug use a separate problem from teenage drinking. *Alcohol is a drug.* In fact, it's America's most widely used mood-altering drug, and the number-one drug of abuse among adolescents.

People assume that since adults can buy alcohol legally, the stuff must be basically harmless. Yet even relatively small amounts of alcohol—say, a few beers—can impair a kid's thinking, judgment, and physical coordination. If the youngster has been having suicidal thoughts, alcohol may lower his inner controls and diminish his judgment so much that he suddenly acts on a suicidal impulse: crashes his car, jumps off a bridge, steps into the path of a moving vehicle. In addition, alcohol is a so-called "gateway" drug for teens. A kid who drinks at parties is quite likely to try marijuana, too. For a kid familiar with marijuana, it seems like a small step to try cocaine, speed, downers, and some other "recreational" drug . . . and so on.

Myth: All kids who try to commit suicide have a problem with drinking or drugs.
Reality: Almost 50 percent of adolescents who commit suicide are reportedly drunk or high shortly before they die, and some 75 percent of kids who try but fail to commit suicide are under the influence at the time of the attempt. Any kid who becomes dependent on alcohol or drugs is at increased risk for suicide—but this does not imply that every suicidal kid is a substance abuser. Some of the youngsters I described in this book were perfectly straight, sober kids who became suicidal because of intolerable depression or what they perceived as unbearable pressure from their parents or society.

Myth: A kid who wants to commit suicide by overdosing has to take a tremendous amount of the drug.
Reality: With certain mixtures of drugs, a relatively small quantity can cause death. For instance, swallowing a bottle full of a barbiturate such as phenobarbital or seconal can itself be fatal; in a person who has been drinking alot of alcohol however; just a few barbiturate pills may prove lethal.

Myth: Marijuana is just a harmless drug that makes people happy. No kid could commit suicide while high on marijuana.
Reality: Marijuana may be fun for a beginning user. For the kid who smokes it a lot, however, marijuana is often a profoundly alienating drug. The chronic "pothead" bumbles and stumbles through life, disconnected from any meaningful involvement with his peers. His self-

absorption, detachment, and loneliness amount to a depression that may become suicidal.

Even when it's only used occasionally, marijuana can be dangerous. For a depressed, vulnerable youngster who has been thinking of suicide, a few beers and a joint at a party may be all it takes to push him over the brink.

Myths About Families and Suicide

Myth: Teenagers who try but fail to commit suicide are just manipulating their parents. If anything, they deserve punishment, not sympathy.
Reality: The so-called suicidal gesture—a self-injurious action that wouldn't have resulted in death—is a kid's way of communicating a feeling of desperation. In that sense, it is indeed manipulative. However, parents who think punishment is the answer are missing the point. The youngster is using dramatic action because she feels she can't communicate her desperation in any other way. She needs help dealing with her own feelings and communicating them effectively. The parents may need this kind of help, too.

Myth: A teenager may commit suicide to get back at parents who were too strict with him.
Reality: "Revenge" suicides occasionally happen, but it's much more common to see a suicide note that says something like, "This isn't your fault. No one is to blame." Inside the mind of the suicidal youngster, the emotional climate is typically one of profound depression, self-loathing, and despair, not revenge. Of course, conflicts with harsh parents may contribute to a youngster's depression. But depression can develop in kids whose parents are extremely strict, or quite lenient—or anywhere in between.

Myth: A child whose teenage brother or sister has gestured or attempted suicide will be careful not to make the same mistake.
Reality: Children are extremely imitative. A small girl who has seen her older sister attract lots of attention with a dramatic, nonfatal suicide gesture may try the same maneuver herself a few years later, if for some reason she finds herself feeling lonely, depressed and desperate.

Myth: There is no such thing as a family tendency toward suicide. Any such family would quickly die out.
Reality: Let's say that a teenage boy is thinking or talking about suicide. As a psychiatrist, I will more strongly consider psychiatric hospitalization if I learn that this boy had a relative who committed suicide. The "family tendency toward suicide" *is* a well-recognized phenomenon. It may be caused by an inherited, biological vulnerability to depression. Or it may be an imitative mechanism, in which the relative who committed suicide implicitly "gave permission" to other family members to respond to difficulties in this way. Possibly it is a combination of both of these factors. In any case, it's not unusual to see family trees dotted with suicides through several generations, without the family "dying out."

Myths About the Suicidal Adolescent's Thoughts

Myth: Talking about suicide will encourage a kid to commit suicide.
Reality: This is probably the most common of all the suicide myths. Everything psychiatrists have learned over the past three decades tells us that you don't make a kid suicidal by bringing up the subject of suicide. In fact, if the youngster has been thinking of suicide, she may be very relieved at the opportunity to discuss this usually taboo subject.

Of course, if you run right up to a kid and blurt out, "You're thinking of suicide, aren't you?" her reaction may be incredulity and contempt. Even if she *has* been having suicidal thoughts, she probably won't feel comfortable about revealing them instantly. It will take time for her to think things over, gain confidence that you are a sympathetic listener, and explain the context of her unhappy feelings.

Myth: Suicide is a crazy thing to do. If a kid commits suicide, it proves he was crazy.
Reality: There is nothing inherently crazy about suicide; many perfectly normal people have occasional fleeting thoughts about it. Often, a person reaches the point of suicide by an almost logical progression. Try to envision an adolescent walking along a high, narrow ledge: life is the wall he can lean on, and death is the abyss he must avoid falling into. Usually his thoughts and feelings are aligned in such a way that he leans more or less strongly on the supportive wall of life. But now suppose that he has to endure a series of setbacks: failure at school; frustration over his looks, weight, or physical development; disappointment over cancelled plans; betrayal by a friend; the death of a beloved relative. If these negatives weigh heavily enough, they can shift the balance so that he starts to lean toward the abyss of death. At this point, we can say that he is at risk for suicide. To topple him over the brink, it may take nothing more than a minor push—for instance, a few beers to lower his inhibitions, plus a sudden opportunity to point a loaded gun at his head. In retrospect, it may even seem that his suicide was frighteningly predictable.

Myth: Once a kid had decided to commit suicide, there is nothing you can do to change her mind.
Reality: On the contrary, the vast majority of suicidal kids have mixed feelings right up to the instant of their suicidal act, and sometimes even beyond. For instance,

nine out of 10 teen suicide attempts take place in the home between 3 p.m. and midnight, when parents or others are most likely to come to the rescue. An adult who can recognize suicidal tendencies in a teenager may be able to prevent her from taking her life.

Myths About the Suicidal Adolescent's Behavior

Myth: If the kid didn't leave a note, it probably wasn't suicide.
Reality: Only 10 to 35 percent of people who commit suicide leave a suicide note. The youngster who kills himself without leaving any message may have been too profoundly depressed and alienated to even consider trying to communicate his thoughts. Or he may have assumed that a note was unnecessary—that everyone would know exactly why he felt he had to take his life. Still another possibility: even if he had been desperately depressed for some time, his final suicidal act may have been an impulsive gesture that didn't allow time for writing a note.

Myth: A kid who talks about committing suicide probably won't do it.
Reality: When a kid talks about committing suicide, you should *always* take it seriously. Often, after a teenage suicide, we hear this kind of comment from friends: "He said he was going to kill himself, but nobody believed him. We thought he was just kidding around."

Myth: A kid who has attempted suicide before probably won't try it again.
Reality: According to one study, up to 65 percent of all people in the United States who kill themselves made one or more previous suicide attempts. If a depressed adolescent tries but fails to commit suicide, and if her underlying depression and despair continue, she may

keep on trying until she actually does take her life. This is why it's important to get competent professional treatment for a youngster who has made a suicide attempt.

Myth: A kid who was talking about suicide, but then cheers up, is definitely out of the danger zone. Reality: Severe, biologically based depression can subdue a kid, making him feel incapable of any action at all. A delicate moment arrives when the physical symptoms of depression begin to lift and energy starts to return. The youngster who still has strong feelings of despair and worthlessness will now have the power to *act* on those feelings. If a very depressed kid suddenly snaps into a state of uncharacteristic cheerfulness, this may be a signal that he has made up his mind to kill himself, now has the energy, and feels relieved that the moment of decision is behind him.

Sources

Cheifets, Philip; Posener, Joel; LaHaye, Andre, et al., "An Epidemiologic Study of Adolescent Suicide," *Canadian Journal of Psychiatry,* vol. 32, November 1987, pp. 656–59.

Crewdson, John, *By Silence Betrayed.* Boston and Toronto: Little, Brown and Company, 1988.

Evans, Glen, and Farberow, Norman L., eds.: *The Encyclopedia of Suicide.* New York: Facts On File, 1988.

Fox, William, with Hynd, Noel, *The Cop and the Kid.* New York: Congdon & Weed, Inc., 1983.

Gardner, Sandra, with Rosenberg, Gary, *Teenage Suicide.* New York: Julian Messner, 1985.

Heacock, Don R., "Suicidal Behavior in Black and Hispanic Youth," *Psychiatric Annals* 20:3, March 1990, pp. 134–42.

Hendin, Herbert, "Youth Suicide: A Psychosocial Perspective," *Suicide and Life-Threatening Behavior* 17:2, Summer 1987, pp. 151–65.

Husain, Syed Arshad, "Current Perspective on the Role of Psychosocial Factors in Adolescent Suicide," *Psychiatric Annals* 20:3, March 1990, pp. 122–27.

Miller, Derek, *Attack on the Self.* Northvale, N. J.: Jason Aronson Inc., 1986.

Newman, Bruce, "The Last Loud Roar," *Sports Illustrated,* May 28, 1990, pp. 54–58.

Pfeffer, Cynthia R., "Clinical Perspectives on Treatment of Suicidal Behavior Among Children and Adolescents," *Psychiatric Annals* 20:3, March 1990, pp. 143–50.

Range, Lillian; Goggin, William, and Steede, Kevin, "Perception of Behavioral Contagion of Adolescent Suicide," *Suicide and Life-Threatening Behavior* 18:4, Winter 1988, pp. 334–41.

Rangell, Leo, "The Decision to Terminate One's Life: Psychoanalytic Thoughts on Suicide," *Suicide and Life-Threatening Behavior* 18:1, Spring 1988, pp. 28–46.

Rush, Florence, *The Best Kept Secrets*. Englewood Cliffs, N. J.: Prentice-Hall, Inc., 1980.

Spurlock, Jeanne, "Adolescent Suicide: Introduction," *Psychiatric Annals* 20:3, March 1990, pp. 120–21.

Thompson, James W., and Walker, R. Dale, "Adolescent Suicide Among American Indians and Alaska Natives," *Psychiatric Annals* 20:3, March 1990, pp. 128–33.

U.S. Department of Health and Human Services: *Report of the National Conference on Youth Suicide (1985), Washington, D.C.* Washington, Youth Suicide National Center, 1985.

Index

Facts About Southwood Hospital

Southwood Hospital and Residential Treatment Centers has been serving the San Diego Community since 1972. Southwood's 104-bed, acute care hospital provides the following programs:

- Child and Young Adolescent Program for ages 4–14
- Adolescent and Dual Diagnosis Program for ages 13–17
- Adult Psychiatric and Dual Diagnosis Program for ages 18+
- Adult Neurobehavior Program for ages 18+
- Adult Sexual Trauma Program for ages 18+

Southwood's 83 bed, 24 hour long-term Residential Treatment Centers provide the following programs:

- Child Program for ages 5–9
- Early Adolescent Program for ages 10–14
- Adolescent and Dual Diagnosis Program for ages 13–17

All programs provide:

- Free Confidential Evaluations and Programs
- Individualized Treatment
- Family Therapy/Parent Support
- Accredited School for Children and Adolescents
- All Programs are Medically Supervised
- All Programs Accredited by the Joint Commission of Hospitals (JCAH)

FOR MORE INFORMATION OR A FREE EVALUATION 24 HOURS

1-800-544-COPE